IRISH POLITICS TODAY

second edition

Neil Collins and Frank McCann

Manchester University Press

Manchester and New York

Distributed exclusively in the USA and Canada by St. Martin's Press

Published by Manchester University Press
Oxford Road, Manchester M13 9PL, UK
and Room 400, 175 Fifth Avenue, New York, NY 10010, USA

Distributed exclusively in the USA and Canada by St. Martin's Press, Inc.,
175 Fifth Avenue, New York, NY 10010, USA

Reprinted with amendments 1993

A catalogue record for this book is available from the British Library

Library of Congress cataloging in publication data applied for

ISBN 0 7190 3645-3 paperback

Typeset in Great Britain
by Koinonia Ltd

Printed in Great Britain
by Biddles Ltd, Guildford & King's Lynn

CONTENTS

NOTE ON THE SECOND EDITION

The process of updating this book has drawn heavily on the goodwill of many of the same colleagues as the first edition. Again we owe them considerable thanks.

We wish to acknowledge the useful and constructive comments of various reviewers and readers. Most notably, we are indebted to Mark Durkan, Dermot Scott, Dennis Kennedy and Reg North for their suggested revisions. Stephen Kelly also provided valuable assistance in preparing this edition.

N. C., F. McC.
April 1991

PREFACE

Irish politics have been presented as too idiosyncratic to understand and beyond the bounds of useful generalisation. In this book, we aim to make Irish politics less of a conundrum and help the reader to see its reasonably comprehensible patterns. Many people have helped us with this book; none is responsible for its content. We would particularly like to acknowledge the contribution to the 'Key facts' section of John Coakley, University of Limerick. Among others who offered advice and to whom we are most grateful are: Brian Farrell, University College Dublin; Paul Arthur, Michael Salter, Kate Stewart and Oonagh Steltox, University of Ulster; Harvey Cox, University of Liverpool; Richard Haslem, University College Cork; and Ruth Delap, Conor Barrington, Seán Dooney and several of their colleagues in the Irish civil service. We thank the series editor Bill Jones and all those at Manchester University Press for their frank and useful comments on the first draft. Margaret McLaughlin, who re-typed the subsequent versions, is also owed our gratitude. There is seldom a right time to finish a book on contemporary politics. Events, such as elections, are rarely ordered to suit authors. Our families, who showed much patience and forbearance are, however, relieved that the writing of this volume is over.

N.C., F.McC.
May 1989

1

IRELAND: WHAT KIND OF STATE?

There are many aspects of life in Ireland that Irish people and visitors regard as special and even unique. Irish politics today are no exception. Irish people at home and abroad are notorious for their interest in politics. The 'heroic' story of Ireland is attested to in a rich tradition of literature, music, myth and involvement in politics. It is easy, therefore, to concentrate on what sets Ireland apart and fail to see it in its wider political and economic context. Indeed, many books on Irish politics present a picture so full of strange parties, scheming clerics and manipulative politicians that it leaves the reader more bemused than informed. Ireland, it seems, is always different. In this chapter, we aim to put Ireland in its rightful and comprehensible place as an interesting example of a small, Western, capitalist, liberal–democratic, post-colonial state trying to resolve problems of a kind common to other such countries, but in the light of its own particular conditions.

History

The island of Ireland contains two jurisdictions, that of Northern Ireland, part of the UK, and the Republic of Ireland. The Republic, which is referred to as Ireland in this book, became politically independent from the UK in 1922 under the title of the Irish Free State. It occupies twenty-six of the thirty-two counties into which the island was administratively divided when the treaty with Britain, setting up the new state, was signed.

The island of Ireland was inhabited comparatively recently.

Until approximately 9,000 years ago it was too cold to be attractive to humans. Since then, however, there have been invasions by several peoples of which the Celts were just one. and each of these has had significant cultural or political influence. In political and institutional terms, the greatest legacy was left by the British. The Tudor state, identified with the Reformation, which had failed to take root in Ireland, stamped its authority firmly on the country. By 1603 English rule had superseded that of the Gaelic chiefs throughout most of the island. Despite periods of resistance, Ireland was effectively subjected to British rule until the years immediately before independence.

Resistance to British rule was frequently influenced by developments abroad, particularly in France and America. When Americans rebelled in the 1770s, Irish parliamentarians, their case strengthened by the existence of a military force of 'Volunteers', pressed for more legislative autonomy for Dublin. Again in 1789, the French Revolution encouraged the open organisation of pressure for radical parliamentary reform and national unity. At the same time the military tradition was also encouraged and in 1798, with the promise of French assistance, Wolfe Tone attempted an overthrow of British rule. Both parliamentary and military action failed to achieve the establishment of more Irish political institutions and, a declared objective of leadership of both, greater unity of purpose between Catholics and Protestants. Indeed the rebellion served more to emphasise the separateness of the two communities.

The bulk of the native Irish population remained Catholic and alienated from what was in effect a British Protestant state in Ireland. The Irish economy was regulated largely in the interest of Britain which was establishing itself as the world's most powerful capitalist country. By the mid-nineteenth century Ireland had a largely stock-rearing and exporting economy and a declining population. Deaths from the Famine in the years 1845–49 were approximately one million and 1.5 million people emigrated. On the other hand, Britain's industrial revolution had made it a manufacturing giant. Only in the north-east of Ireland, where there was a settler and Protestant majority, did industry flourish.

From 1800 Ireland was governed from London through a cabinet minister, the Irish Chief Secretary. Irish constituencies returned members to the British parliament at Westminster on a franchise system similar to England's. Modern democratic institutions, such as a disciplined parliamentary group and mass party organisation, developed during the nineteenth century. The major Irish leaders were Daniel O'Connell and Charles Stewart Parnell. O'Connell sought the removal of anti-Catholic laws. Parnell advocated land reform and home rule. Both set new standards in political oratory and parliamentary manoeuvres. Neither O'Connell nor Parnell achieved their final aims but they laid the foundations of popular respect for parliamentary democracy. Their legacy is attested to by the primary place given to parliamentary institutions by later Irish leaders and the acceptance of the transfers of power that have taken place since independence, even after the bitterness of the Civil War.

The Great Famine

The population of Ireland almost doubled between 1800 and 1847. The 1841 census recorded a population of almost eight million. Almost one-third of the Irish were living at a below subsistence level, depending for their diet almost exclusively on the potato crop. The Great Famine resulted from the failure of the potato crop in successive years from 1845 to 1851. Over one million people died of starvation and emigration reached massive proportions. By 1911, the Irish population was 4.4 million.

The Great Famine had major impacts on Irish social structures, patterns of landholding and commerce. It also created a large and embittered American diaspora of Irish rural origin.

Towards the end of the nineteenth century, democratic local government and a public service based on the principles of merit recruitment were established in Ireland, along British lines. By the first decade of the twentieth century Catholics in Ireland enjoyed the same level of welfare, educational and property rights as any citizen of the UK. Only in the most senior public positions were the Anglo-Irish Protestant elite still firmly entrenched.

Independence

By the final decade of the nineteenth century the popular sentiment for what was called 'home rule' was expressed mainly through the Irish Parliamentary Party, which had a clear majority of seats in Ireland. Using their numerical strength and the pivotal voting role it gave them in a British parliament split between Conservatives and Liberals, the Irish Party eventually managed to secure the Home Rule Act by September 1914. The First World War had, however, started in August and the implementation of the Act was postponed, pending the outcome of the war. The initiative in the campaign for some form of independence passed out of the hands of the parliamentarians during the course of the war.

Home rule

This involved the restoration to Ireland of a parliament, subordinate in certain respects to the British government, but with general autonomy over domestic legislation. From 1870 onwards home rule became a rallying call for those Irish hostile to British rule. Home Rule Bills, introduced by the British Liberal Prime Minister Gladstone, giving Ireland limited self-government within the Empire, were defeated in the UK parliament. The Third Home Rule Bill, introduced in April 1912 by Asquith's Liberal government, was passed in September 1914, but its operation was suspended because of the First World War.

The militant tradition of Irish patriotism, which had always found expression in armed conflict, gained the upper hand following a seemingly abortive coup in 1916. When the war ended the British authorities were dealing with more radical and militant politicians, whose party, Sinn Féin, won an overwhelming majority of seats at the 1918 general election. These MPs formed a parliament in Dublin in 1919 called Dáil Eireann, the political arm of an independence movement which the British tried to suppress in an armed struggle which ended in 1921 in the negotiated partition of Ireland. The Irish Free State was established in twenty-six counties while a separate administration was formed in the six north-eastern counties (see Chapter 7). This Anglo-Irish Treaty of 1921 had a decisive effect on the development of Irish politics. As will be seen in more detail in Chapter 3, Sinn Féin split over the Treaty and a civil war between the two sides followed. The two main present-day political parties in Ireland, Fianna Fáil, which opposed the Treaty and Fine Gael, which supported it, have their roots in this division.

Institutions

The political institutions of Ireland, which will be examined in more detail in subsequent chapters, are for the most part based on those in Britain. On its formation in 1922, the Irish state inherited an almost complete set of state institutions. Without undue delay, arrangements were made to cope with new tasks, such as defence and foreign affairs. Compared to many other newly-independent states, at an institutional level Ireland had a very smooth transfer of power.

The Constitution

In 1937 a new written constitution was adopted when de Valera, chief of the anti-treaty forces and leader of Fianna Fáil, was Taoiseach (Prime Minister). The principal features of the Constitution are:

    (a) The republican nature of the state, with a non-executive

President as Head though the Republic was not declared until 1948;

(b) the unitary nature of the state: the state parliament is the supreme law-making body, though it must not enact laws repugnant to the Constitution and has since 1973 had to take account of European Community obligations;

(c) separation of powers: the organs of government are divided threefold into executive, legislative and judicial, each with limited and distinct functions;

(d) a bicameral legislature: the Oireachtas, composed of an upper house, Seanad Eireann, and a lower house, Dáil Eireann; the President is also part of the Oireachtas;

(e) a government to carry out executive functions within the constraints of the Constitution and law; and

(f) courts, which incorporate the judicial power; the court of final appeal is called the Supreme Court.

All of the institutions, presidency, Oireachtas, government and courts, were given specific powers to be exercised within the general principles of a British-style parliamentary democracy, though the Constitution does have some non-British features such as judicial review (see below). Thus some important conventions were not stated explicitly. Even political parties were not formally recognised. Nevertheless, the fact that the Constitution is a written document does mean that governments and legislators must act within its provisions. Some of these are very general and reflect the social thinking, and in particular that of the Catholic Church, of the mid-1930s. Article 44 recognised the special position of the Catholic Church although this has since been deleted. The courts are the final arbiters of a law's constitutionality. The only method for altering provisions of the Constitution is by referendum. There have been twelve proposed changes since 1959, when the first referendum was held (see Chapter 2).

As will be shown in Chapter 2, it may be that the Constitution and the system of law it outlines will change at an accelerating rate over the next few years. The Constitution specifically allowed continuity of statutes and common law provided this was not inconsistent with its provisions. Such inconsistencies have arisen but on the whole there has been a tendency for Irish legislators and judges to look to Britain for ideas on statute and precedent. Recently, however, there has been a greater willingness to be innovative and independent, particularly among the judiciary. Irish politics today are thus becoming less 'British', as politicians, bureaucrats, jurists and others reflect the broader influences of over sixty-five years of self-government and wider foreign experience.

The European Community

A major boost to this process has been Ireland's membership of the European Community (EC), which has led to Irish institutions having to accommodate wider considerations than before. As will be outlined in later chapters, the EC and its governing treaties effectively introduced a new source of laws, policies and court rulings into Irish politics. Beyond the institutional influences, domestic and European, Ireland has increased its openness to change through a conscious expansion of its trading relations. The inexorable influences of the world economic order are now clearly felt.

Ireland in the world economy

The world economy can usefully be divided into three areas:the *core*, the *periphery* and the *semi-periphery*. Core countries are those colonial powers of the nineteenth century such as Britain, France and the Netherlands, together with countries like Germany, the USA and Japan, which achieved economic success without long-lasting colonial acquisitions. In these core countries much of the wealth of the world is concentrated. The multinational companies are based there, as is the finance necessary for economic development. These countries receive the bulk of the profits generated in the economies of the rest of the world.

The periphery is made up of those countries commonly known as the 'Third World'. The core group relies upon the periphery for many of the raw materials necessary for its industry and some of its food. In turn the countries in the periphery are usually dependent on the production of minerals or a single crop for their export earnings. Often a peripheral country is economically tied to a single core country, such as is the case with the Philippines or Honduras with the USA and several Francophone African countries with France. The semi-periphery group are intermediate in status. These countries are not as dependent as the periphery group. They have a much more diversified economic structure and in them industrialisation is well advanced. To a significant extent industry is locally owned and financed. Wage rates and living standards are higher than in the periphery. Countries often move into the intermediate group through strategies designed to increase their industrial sector substantially. But since these countries do not possess sufficient wealth for such development strategies, they obtain the finance from multinationals. These large international enterprises locate in the semi-periphery because of the relatively high levels of skill in the work-force, developed infrastructure, such as roads and communications, lower wage rates than in the core and financial inducements from government. This threefold model of the world economy will help us to understand Ireland's current position as a small semi-peripheral capitalist state with a large agricultural sector. The aim of the capitalist state is to provide the conditions for the functioning of an economy which is largely owned by private (non-state) organisations and individuals. In doing this it is constrained by the conditions operating in the international market system.

The Irish economy before independence

Up until the Act of Union which in 1800 linked Ireland and Britain, Ireland had its own independent parliament with the power to regulate trade. With the union of the two countries under one parliament at Westminster, the two islands became a free-trading area. Several Irish industries which were protected, such as leather, silk, glass, hardware, furniture and wool, continued to have some of their produce protected by a 10 per cent tax for twenty years or so. By 1824, however, all duties had been abolished. Ireland, with its lack of large resources of raw materials, was at a great disadvantage compared to England. The Irish economy became fully integrated into the free-trading and industrialised economy of Britain. It remained underdeveloped, with the majority of the population dependent on agriculture. One of the most important demands that Sinn Féin pushed in their negotiations with the British in 1921 was control over Ireland's economy. The Treaty did not establish a completely independent republic of the whole of the island of Ireland, as Sinn Féin had wanted. Many Irish people were willing to accept this compromise in the short term because they had won full fiscal and economic freedom. It had long been a central argument of Sinn Féin that Ireland's poverty and consequent high emigration could be explained by British economic policy in the country. Now that they had control over their own economic affairs they would put their ideas into action. When Sinn Féin split into two because of the Treaty, each opposing side contained a mix of opinion on economic policy. The pro-Treaty group, Cumann na nGaedheal, which held office until 1932, tended to have more free-traders than did the anti-Treaty group. The emphasis of the first Irish government was thus on free trade.

The economy after independence

In 1900 the main characteristics of the Irish economy were its dependence on agriculture and, more particularly, the export of live cattle to Britain. By the outbreak of the First World War Ireland enjoyed almost a monopoly position in supplying the British market with agricultural produce. After the war this prosperous situation was not sustained. Irish agricultural exports declined sharply in the face of competition from Denmark, New Zealand and elsewhere. The new Irish government took action to help recover export markets, especially those in Britain. In the short term the results were impressive. The export of produce such as eggs and butter increased dramatically, contributing to an overall increase in the size of agricultural exports. This situation was to be changed, however, by events in Britain.

The economic crisis of the 1920s and 1930s

The British economy, as a key part of the world economy, underwent an economic crisis in the final years of the 1920s because of the collapse in the world financial markets. The British government reacted by erecting barriers to imports into Britain, and by 1932 a general tariff on imports had been introduced. The British market was restricted by government measures in the interests of its own farmers. Ireland, too, had been affected by the general world recession and had imposed tariffs on imports such as butter, oats and bacon.

Protectionism

A change of government in 1932 signalled Ireland's move from free-trade principles to protectionism. This change had political as well as economic causes. The image of Ireland as a largely rural country made up of small owner-run farms ran deep in the new government party, Fianna Fáil. De Valera, the party's founder and leader, outlined Fianna Fáil's approach in a famous broadcast on St Patrick's Day 1943:

That Ireland, which we dreamed of, would be the home of a people who valued material wealth as the basis of right living, of a people who were satisfied with frugal comfort and devoted their leisure to the things of the spirit – a land whose countryside would be bright with cosy homesteads, whose fields and villages would be joyous with the sound of industry, with the romping of sturdy children, the contest of athletic youths and the laughter of comely maidens, whose firesides would be forums for the wisdom of serene old age. It would, in a word, be the home of a people living the life that God desires that man should live.[1]

Fianna Fáil took office in 1932. While in opposition they had developed a policy of economic self-sufficiency. This was to be achieved by protecting the domestic markets from imports, to give Irish producers a better chance of becoming established. As we have seen, world events favoured this approach. The emphasis of the new government was the reverse of that of the old. Whereas formerly a producer had to argue a case for protection, now protection was to be given unless a case could be made against it. In 1932 the Emergency Imposition of Duties Act allowed the Irish Government to impose, vary or revoke any customs duties it wished. Within a few months Ireland became one of the most heavily tariffed countries in the world. Imports of some 1,947 articles were controlled by 1937. The 1930s were very difficult years for Irish farmers as the government tried to diversify production behind trade barriers. A system of guaranteed prices with restrictions on imports brought an emphasis on food crops for home consumption. Agricultural employment and output fell from their 1926 levels of 52 and 32 per cent respectively to 48 per cent of total employment and 27 per cent of output by 1938. To add to these problems there was a short acrimonious trade dispute with Britain known as 'the economic war' over land annuity payments. This was the money paid to Britain by Irish farmers buying out their land under the Land Acts of the nineteenth century. The Irish government refused to hand this money over to the British. Britain responded by imposing high tariffs on Irish exports to the UK. This row ended in 1938 with an agreement under which tariffs between the two countries were reduced. Further, the residual naval facilities Britain had in Ireland (under the 1921 Treaty) were handed over to Irish control. This concession was soon to have significant military consequences for the UK.

The Second World War

The outbreak of the Second World War in September 1939 had serious implications for Ireland, even though the country remained technically neutral. Access to foods from abroad was restricted, so there was a very substantial increase in the production of crops for home consumption. In the 'Emergency' years of the Second World War the Irish acres under tillage vastly increased. In contrast, the output of livestock and livestock products fell, as access to export markets decreased. Exports to Britain continued throughout the war.

Post-war changes

After the War the European countries, with the aid of the USA's Marshall Plan, set about the rebuilding of their shattered economies. A study of the Irish economy concluded that Ireland's main contribution to European recovery would be in the production of food for export. Ireland's official economic programme for the period 1949–53 accepted this as the primary policy.

Despite Ireland's fairly successful attempts to industrialise by encouraging an influx of foreign capital in the 1960s, agriculture has retained its importance in the Irish economy. In 1986 agriculture made up 19 per cent of domestic merchandise exports and accounted for 11 per cent of the net national product and 17 per cent of employment. The average comparative figures for the European Community were 4 and 8 per cent respectively. But such figures mask the change in the farming community.

The protectionist regime lasted up until the 1950s when there was a general shift towards the liberalising of trade. By the early 1960s it was believed that Ireland would soon be in the EC and would have to open up its industries to competition. The UK and Ireland eventually became members of the EC in 1973, but they had already formed a free-trade area between themselves in July 1966. Before 1973 the European Common Agricultural Policy (CAP) had virtually closed Community markets to Irish cattle and beef: 'The principal aspirations of post-war agricultural policy have been largely met by Ireland's accession to the EC. The original emphasis in the CAP on security of food supply has provided access for Irish agricultural products to a large market, with the bonus of price guarantees for certain major products ... '.[2]

The growth of agriculture

Farming prospered between 1970 and 1978 as the over-reliance on British markets decreased. The volume of agricultural output rose at almost 4 per cent per annum, the highest recorded rate of prolonged growth. Since then Irish agriculture has enjoyed more fluctuating fortune and greater uncertainty. The factors which will determine the future are largely outside the control of Irish governments. What is likely to continue is the process by which some farms become larger, more efficient and commercially run, while many remain small, inefficient and unable to sustain their owners' families without substantial government and European Community help. De Valera's dream of a rural Ireland made up mainly of family-owned and worked farms has been gradually eroded by world market conditions and the policies of successive Irish governments.

Rapid structural changes have been a feature of the last fifteen years, due largely to income relativity, as between agriculture and the rest of the economy, being influenced by the EC-determined price policies. Also, the efficiency of Irish agriculture has greatly increased through the application of technology and improved management skills, both influenced by EC farm investment policies. Current Irish agricultural policy has to be framed mainly in the light of the provisions of the CAP, which is, in effect, a framework of agricultural rules for the twelve member states. Through its price support arrangements and market management functions, the CAP influences and largely determines the market conditions under which Irish farm output is produced and sold.[3]

The changing policy in the Republic of Ireland from protection to free trade was a result of more than just the change in world opinion. The 1950s was a time of increasing economic difficulty and political uncertainty in Ireland. In the six years between 1948 and 1954 there were three general elections, of which a coalition of anti-Fianna Fáil parties won the first and the third. Increasing unemployment, with the consequent increases in poverty and emigration, put Fianna Fáil under considerable pressure. Within the party, the feeling emerged that protection and self-sufficiency had been tried and had failed. A new approach had to be considered if Fianna Fáil's guiding role in Irish politics was to survive. Though the critique of existing strategies had developed over some years, a change of party leader in 1959 facilitated a change in direction when de Valera was succeeded by the much more pragmatic Seán Lemass.

Foreign investment

The essential thrust of the new policy was the opening of the Irish economy to foreign capital. Agricultural employment was declining. The commercialisation of farming would increase the trend to a capital-intensive agriculture. The industries protected by tariffs and quotas had become less efficient rather than more so. They had failed to absorb the loss of employment from the land and would have to be encouraged to expand by other means. The main aim of the new policy was to increase industrial development by encouraging multinational firms to set up business in Ireland. It was hoped that foreign investment would increase employment, create an expanding domestic market and improve the balance of payments. Exports would be encouraged because most multinationals produce for an international market. It was also believed that the needs of the new foreign firms would provide opportunities for new Irish businesses.

Industrialisation

The initial achievements of the new policy certainly seem impressive. Foreign-owned firms operating in Ireland created 22,000 jobs in the period 1973-80 and now employ around 80,000 people in the country, about 34 per cent of the manufacturing workforce. Ireland has not, however, developed into a 'core' economy. The jobs which foreign firms have tended to provide in Ireland are largely unskilled or semi-skilled. In areas of high technology, such as engineering, many foreign firms import components simply for assembly in Ireland. Though there are hopeful signs of a changing pattern, many educated men and women still have to emigrate if they wish to enjoy the living standards to which they aspire. Further, most of the foreign firms are too capital intensive to reduce unemployment as much as hoped. The average cost of each new job created by foreign industry has been high. Lastly, not enough foreign firms have located in the poorer regions to make a significant impact there.

Employment

Although the industrial sector of the Irish economy has been
making an increasing contribution to the wealth of the country, it
has not created full employment. Industry's contribution to gross
domestic product has risen over 10 per cent in the last two
decades, which more than compensates for the decline in agriculture of almost 8 per cent. But the employment picture is less
encouraging. Industrial employment has only increased by 7 per
cent while agricultural employment has decreased by a substantial
16 per cent. Ireland's industrial strategy, pursued since the 1960s,
has thus failed to live up to expectations in solving the problems of
wealth creation, unemployment and regional imbalances.

Regional policy

One of the major characteristics of the world economic system is
the development of regional imbalances in wealth and opportunities. Where market forces are allowed to determine the location of
industry and commerce, wealth will tend to be concentrated in
certain areas. Under-employment, low wages, high dependence on
social security payments, poverty and emigration are endemic in
some places, while prosperity is concentrated elsewhere. In Ireland the further west and north one travels from Dublin the worse
the economic conditions become. In common with others, Irish
governments have sought to generate policies to counteract the
economic forces leading to over concentration of economic activity. Until late 1988 there was, however, no indigenous regional
policy for Ireland after accession to the EC.

In an effort to tackle the problem of regional imbalance the six
original members of the EC agreed to set a ceiling of 20 per cent
on the amount of government assistance for investment projects in
the more prosperous regions. Following enlargement of the
Community, the system of ceilings was extended in 1975. The
regions were divided into four groups. In the first group were the
rich regions, for which the 20 per cent ceiling continued to apply.
The poorest regions formed a group for which there was no

ceiling, as long as other Community principles were not breached. This group includes both the Republic and Northern Ireland. To provide aid for poorer regions the European Regional Development Fund (ERDF) was established.

The ERDF money is a welcome addition to investment in Ireland though most of it has been spent in the relatively developed areas. It does not come near the amount needed to reverse their relative decline. The Fund itself and Ireland's share of it are too small. A significant transfer of resources between Community countries would be needed to reverse the movement of wealth to the 'core' areas of Europe. The political will (in the richer countries) has not until recently been sufficient for such a transfer of resources. The EC has now come to place greater emphasis on 'cohesion' or more equal sharing of economic opportunities and success. Today the whole of Ireland has less than 75 per cent of the average per capita income for the Community but, as part of the preparations for the development of the internal market set for 1992, European leaders have agreed to double the so-called 'Structural Fund' which includes the ERDF, the Social Fund and the guidance section of the Agricultural Fund.

The European Monetary System

An important part of a country's economic management is its exchange-rate policy. Ireland's currency had always been linked to sterling (except for a period between 1797 and 1826). Thus Ireland's monetary policy was always decided by Britain. Because of the link between the two currencies, the high British inflation of the 1970s had an adverse effect on Ireland. There was little that Irish governments could do to remedy the situation while the link with sterling remained. When discussions began on the setting up of the European Monetary System (EMS), Ireland showed immediate interest. The Irish pound has been part of the EMS since 1979 and is no longer directly linked to sterling, though the UK's currency joined the system in 1990. While this development has had beneficial effects on inflation, it has further decreased the ability of Irish governments to resist the movement of wealth to

European core countries. The EMS decision aptly demonstrates the limits to the 'independence' of a small, economically underdeveloped nation.

Conclusion

We have seen in this chapter that in economic terms the world we live in is a highly integrated system. It is this economic system which to a large extent determines the position of any particular country in the wealthy core, the poor periphery or somewhere in between in the semi-periphery. Ireland fits into this latter sector. Although it is not as wealthy as other parts of western Europe it is certainly not as poor as Third World countries. There is also another significant difference between the Republic of Ireland and many other newly-independent states of the twentieth century. It has remained a stable, liberal democracy with fair and competitive elections, alternating parties in government, an independent judiciary and unchallenged civilian control of the military. Essentially, this is because of the dominant influences on the political actors who led the Irish independence movement.

One of the strongest influences on this elite was the parliamentary tradition. Ireland was directly linked to the British parliament and sent its representatives there. Its political leaders and people were not only schooled in this tradition but used parliament to pursue home rule. Even when the more militant independence movement developed in the second decade of the twentieth century, its parliamentarian outlook was unquestionable. When it withdrew from Westminster it set up its own parliament, Dáil Eireann, in Ireland. One of the reasons why the War of Independence was partially successful was because its leaders gained popular support by way of parliamentary methods.

The parliamentary tradition was all the stronger because the roots of Irish republicanism stretched back to the idea of the French and American revolutions, that power resides in the people and must be exercised on their behalf by the elected representatives. What marks Ireland out from many of the countries which have gone through violent independence struggles in this century is the consensus, even among the different factions of the independence movement, regarding the form of government which they wished to adopt.

Another reason why Ireland has retained its parliamentary tradition lies in the fact that its independence has been achieved almost purely by the struggle of its own people and without the intervention of other major powers. This made the post-independence period in Ireland less violent than in many other countries.

The elements of continuity in the political system, such as the civil service, local government and administration of justice, had an important stabilising effect on the newly-independent Ireland. The most potentially disruptive influence on Irish politics today remains the major unresolved question of the 1922 settlement – Northern Ireland. (The politics of Northern Ireland will be outlined in Chapter 7.) The new Irish Free State was one in which there were few social divisions which might have become reflected in the party political system. Potentially important social divisions had been subsumed under the nationalist struggle. Most Irish people saw political independence as the first step in achieving their own individual or sectional interests. It might have been expected that these divisions would find political expression after independence had been secured. In the event, because the nationalist struggle did not achieve its aims in full, attitudes towards the 1922 settlement remained an important political issue. Chapter 3 will examine how the political system had adapted to other predominantly economic issues to give Ireland its distinctive line-up of parties. Before that, however, the constitutional and legal framework of Irish politics today is outlined in Chapter 2.

References

1 M. Moynihan (ed.), *Speeches and Statements of de Valera*, Dublin: Gill & Macmillan, 1980, pp. 466–9.

2 Seán Dooney, *Irish Agriculture*, Dublin: Institute of Public Administration, 1988, p. 6.

3 *Ibid.*, p. 6.

Further reading

B. Chubb, *The Government and Politics of Ireland*, London: Longman, 1982.

R. Foster, *Modern Ireland 1600–1972*, London: Allen Lane, 1988.

B. Girvin, *Between Two Worlds: Politics and Economy in Independent Ireland*, Dublin: Gill & Macmillan, 1989.

K. Kennedy, T. Giblin & D. McHugh, *The Economic Development of Ireland in the Twentieth Century*, London: Routledge, 1988.

J. Lee, *Ireland 1912–1985, Politics and Society*, Cambridge: Cambridge University Press, 1989.

2
PARTIES, ELECTIONS AND ELECTORATES

Virtually all liberal democracies have competing political parties. In most European countries these parties are based on social distinctions or cleavages, such as class, language or religion. In the Republic of Ireland, the party system reflects no obvious social divisions. Ireland is similar to America in that the parties stand on their records rather than their position on an ideological spectrum. Before independence there were two distinct groups on the island,

---

The Irish language

Irish is the first national language under the terms of Bunreacht na hEireann. The Constitution recognises English as a second official language. Irish is spoken as a first language, however, only in areas known as the Gaeltacht, situated mainly along the western seaboard. According to the 1981 census there are about one million Irish speakers in the Republic. This figure, 31.6 per cent of the population, is a vast overestimate of those who can speak Irish competently and actually use it regularly. Ireland is a predominantly English-speaking country. Nevertheless, the language remains an important part of Irish culture. Many non-Irish speakers support attempts to safeguard its place in education, broadcasting and official business. Several national agencies have been formed to encourage or preserve the use of the language.

differentiated by culture, religion, language and class. These divisions provided the basis for the difference in attitude of the two groups to national independence. To understand the development of the Irish party system we must examine how the struggle for national independence became dominated largely by the Catholic, Gaelic Irish.

The historical basis of the party system

From the end of the seventeenth century the strategy used by the British to secure their rule in Ireland was one of plantation. This involved the replacement of the natives in positions of economic and political power by people brought from Britain. The massive changes in the ownership of land brought about by the plantations has been an enduring cause of social bitterness and political dissent right up to the present day.

Along with the policy of plantation, attempts were made to integrate the Irish forcibly into the English way of life. The Gaelic language and culture were suppressed, as was the Catholic religion. This policy created great animosity between the natives and those they regarded as invaders. The conflict between the planters and the natives was further exacerbated by the struggle for the British Crown between the Protestant forces of William of Orange and the Catholic armies of James II. William's victory at the Battle of the Boyne in 1690 assured Protestant ascendancy in Ireland.

Catholic emancipation and the rise of nationalism

The struggle for Catholic emancipation reached its height in 1829 when the rights of Catholics to vote for and sit in the parliament at Westminster were secured. Although Irish Catholics were a small group in the UK parliament, Irish Protestants realised that their representatives would be swamped in any future Irish Parliament by Catholic members. Despite their political gains, Catholic disaffection with British rule continued. Their economic problems had not been alleviated by integration with Britain. Indeed, free trade made it much more difficult for Irish industry to survive against the competition of the large-scale and well established British firms.

In agriculture, neither free trade nor the achievement of widespread farm ownership solved farmers' problems, such as the smallness of their plots and the lack of investment. These factors led to such inefficient production that many families were barely able to subsist on their farms. Over 8½ million people were locked into this subsistence economy when a succession of crop failures resulted in widespread famine in the mid-1840s. About one million people died of starvation and a further 1,500,000 emigrated. The extent of the 'Great Famine' left an indelible mark on the Irish. The significance of land and landownership to Irish politics was further reinforced.

The vast majority of native tenant farmers became owners under a series of Land Acts in the last quarter of the nineteenth century. Today, 90 per cent of Irish farmers own their land – the highest proportion in the European Community. They achieved ownership after a period of intense agitation led by radical nationalists against the Protestant landowning class. Nationalism and Catholicism became synonymous at grass-roots level. For Catholics, it became clear that Ireland must have its own parliament with the ability to regulate its trade with Britain if it was to develop economically.

The difference in attitude to British rule between the Protestants, mostly concentrated in the north-east, and the great majority of the population was expressed by new Irish political parties. The general election of 1868 was the last in Ireland to be dominated by the English party labels. By 1885 only two parties took seats. The shades of political opinion in Ireland had been reduced to pro- or anti-union with Britain. Those who wanted home rule for Ireland were led by Charles Stewart Parnell. The strategy of the Parnellites at Westminster was to offer support to whichever English party would help the Irish claim for its own parliament.

It was the Liberal Party, with the support of Irish MPs, which dominated Westminster in the decades at the turn of the century. In 1886 Gladstone, the Prime Minister, introduced a Home Rule

Bill. It was defeated at Westminster, when ninety-three Liberals voted against it and the party lost office. In 1893 Gladstone, back in government, brought forward his second Home Rule Bill. It too was defeated, this time in the House of Lords, the British upper chamber. After the retirement of Parnell, following a personal scandal, the Irish nationalist MPs at Westminster formed the Irish Parliamentary Party (IPP). In 1912 Asquith introduced the third Home Rule Bill which was passed, but the IPP, under the leadership of John Redmond, agreed that the Bill should not come into effect until after the First World War.

The Easter Rising

The dominance of the IPP as the voice of Irish nationalism was seriously challenged by more radical politicians at this time. Some of these led an abortive coup in Dublin on Easter Monday 1916. The 'Rising' may not have been a mass or popular affair, but

---

'1916' - The Easter Rising

The Easter Rising of April 1916 marked the beginning of the military campaign for independence. The Rising was an initial failure involving about 2,000 insurrectionists, mainly in Dublin. A few hundred people were killed and much damage done in Dublin city centre. Public reaction, as far as can be judged by contemporary Dublin papers, was initially hostile. It began to favour the militants following the execution of their leaders and the internment of many others. At the 1918 general election militants, under the banner of Sinn Féin, routed the more moderate Irish Party.

Though now subject to more critical historical analysis, the 1916 Easter Rising has a major symbolic importance in Ireland. The 'heroic failure' is still seen by many Nationalists as the 'blood sacrifice' that was necessary to reawaken the Irish to a sense of their nationality.

Britain's extended trial and execution of its leaders swung public sympathy behind the militant wing of the nationalists. In October 1917 the militants' party, Sinn Féin, was reorganised and radicalised, shifting its aim of a dual monarchy to that of an independent republic. In the general election of 1918 Sinn Féin gained seventy-three seats, leaving only six seats to the IPP. The seventy-three Sinn Féin MPs refused to take their seats at Westminster and instead constituted themselves into a Parliament of Ireland (Dáil Eireann) in January 1919. The British government proscribed the Dáil in September 1919 and arrested some of its members, but it continued to meet in secret.

The War of Independence

For the next few years a guerrilla campaign or 'War of Independence' was waged against the British in Ireland. In May 1921 a general election was held for the two parliaments set up in Ireland by the Government of Ireland Act 1920. In the south all the seats were uncontested. Sinn Féin took 124 of them and the remaining four went to independents from Trinity College Dublin. This result strengthened the resolve of the nationalists and undermined Britain's position. In July 1921 the War of Independence came to an end with a truce and in December the Anglo-Irish Treaty was signed between members of Sinn Féin and the British government. This set up the Irish Free State in twenty-six counties of the island, with dominion status under the British Crown.

The Civil War

The Treaty divided Sinn Féin. Those who agreed with it believed it was as much as could be won at that time and laid the basis for eventually securing an independent all-Ireland state. After an acrimonious debate the Treaty was passed by the Dáil, sixty-four votes to fifty-seven. A general election was held in 1922 and the result was a clear majority for acceptance of the Treaty. The anti-Treatyites, under the leadership of Eamon de Valera, won only thirty-six out of 128 seats. Twelve days after the election civil war broke out between the opposing sides. More than 600 lives were lost and the Civil War created divided loyalties and animosities which lasted for decades. The war ended in May 1923 when the anti-Treaty forces laid down their arms, although they refused to accept the legitimacy of the government. The division in Sinn Féin over the Treaty, and the Civil War which resulted, provided the basis for the party system in the Free State. However, as we will see below, the Civil War 'split' itself reflects older divisions.

The break-up of Sinn Féin

In April 1923 the pro-Treaty deputies organised themselves into a new party under the name of Cumann na nGaedheal (League of the Gaels). Membership was open to anyone who supported the Treaty and the new Constitution. At the election in August 1923 this party won only sixty-three seats, with 39 per cent of the vote cast. The anti-Treatyites, or Republicans, were reorganised by de Valera to fight the election under the name Sinn Féin. Its electoral programme consisted of an outright refusal to sit in the Dáil or accept the Free State. It won 27.4 per cent of the total vote and forty-four seats at the election.

The Irish party-political system had been dominated since the 1880s by the demand for legislative independence from Britain. It was the Catholics, who had suffered most under British rule, who supported independence. The effect of the struggle for this was to create a cross-class alliance among Catholics. Latent class divisions were to become more obvious in the divide within the nationalist camp because of the Treaty. In general, the Treaty was supported by those who had most to gain from continued links with the British Commonwealth. These were the former business class, the merchants and 'large' farmers. The Treaty preserved trade links with Britain and bolstered their economic and political position within Ireland. These groups supported Cumann na nGaedheal which, as the government between 1923 and 1932, followed a policy of free trade to protect Ireland's markets in Britain. In 1926, 97 per cent of Irish exports went to the UK (including

Northern Ireland) and 76 per cent of imports came from there.

After the formation of the Irish Free State many of the smallholders, landless farmers and farm labourers gave their support to the anti-Treaty forces, partly because of their long-term aim of making Ireland economically self-sufficient. Such a policy was to involve price supports for agricultural products, in much the same way that the European Community does today. This would guarantee the incomes of small producers. The second, and major, plank in this strategy was industrial development. Once again, this was to be achieved by protecting the domestic market from overseas competition. This attracted the support of small business entrepreneurs whose firms stood a greater chance of survival when protected against the lower-priced goods of overseas companies. It also won the support of a large number of industrial workers as employment opportunities would be increased. Thus the Civil War division, reflected in the emerging party system, did have some social basis.

The rise of Fianna Fáil

The anti-Treaty leader, de Valera, resigned from Sinn Féin and founded a new party, Fianna Fáil (Soldiers of Destiny), in 1926. When the new party fought the general election in June 1927 it won forty-four seats, while the remnants of Sinn Féin (which followed a policy of not taking its seats in the Dáil) only won five. Fianna Fáil claimed most of its support from the less well-off sections of Irish society. Unlike Cumann na nGaedheal, the party in government, Fianna Fáil concentrated on building up a strong organisation based on constituency *cumainn* (party clubs). Further, Fianna Fáil developed policies which seemed more attuned to Ireland's needs after the world-wide economic crisis of the late 1920s. In particular, Fianna Fáil argued for protecting domestic markets.

At the general election in 1932 Fianna Fáil increased its vote by almost 10 per cent and formed a minority government with support from the Labour Party. Fianna Fáil made further gains at the next election in 1933 and was able to remain in office. Indeed it did so for an unbroken run until 1948. As the government for this lengthy period it was able to consolidate and extend its basis of support, through its economic policy of protectionism and its welfare policies, particularly the introduction of unemployment benefit. It was in these years that Fianna Fáil developed into a 'catch-all' party, drawing its support from all sections of Irish society.

Social cleavages and politics

Social cleavages formed the basis of many of the party systems in Europe, so why is Ireland different? In part it is because of the homogeneity of its social structure, for what divisions did exist were comparatively slight. This had a lot to do with the timing and result of the struggle for independence. It took place when the country was industrially undeveloped. There was a relatively small section of the work-force which could have been described as an industrial proletariat. Further, the industrial heartland of the island, Belfast, was severed from the Free State in the Government of Ireland Act in 1920. Secondly, the Land Acts, which allowed farmers to buy their farms, produced a conservative 'landed peasantry'. Although the problems remained in agriculture, farm owners would not contemplate government interference in their work practices or the allocation of land. Thirdly, a social cleavage which is reflected in several party systems in Europe, that of cultural–linguistic differences, is slight in Ireland. The main cleavage, between the Northern Protestant Unionists and the Southern Catholic Nationalists, had been removed by the division of the country into two separate states. Within the Free State the English language was almost universally spoken. The Irish-speaking communities of the Gaeltacht did not constitute a group with a distinct political identity.

A further cause for divisions in other European nations, differences over religion, has little relevance in Ireland. Again, the drawing of the border around the six northern counties left the Free State remarkably homogeneous in terms of religion, around 90 per cent of its population being Catholic. Additionally, the fact

that the Church had sided with the struggle for independence
removed the possibility of church–state conflict and with it the
chance of a political party campaigning for secularisation. Though
there is an important element of Catholic dissent in Irish political
culture, anti–clericalism of the kind found in some other European
countries is absent.

In many countries organised labour or trade unions formed the
basis of a major party appealing for support from the working
classes. In Ireland, the leaders of labour after 1916 did not share
the idea of revolutionary class struggle. National independence
was the dominant political issue. The trade union leaders were
more concerned with building their organisations and increasing
membership. They stayed clear of 'politics', concentrating instead
on the bread–and–butter issues such as pay and working conditions.

The political wing of the labour movement, the Labour Party,
was more a collection of individuals than a mass electoral machine.
They too were politically conservative. The growth in the nationalist movement, given impetus by the 1916 Rising, prevented
the Irish working class becoming an independent force in the
nationalist struggle. The success of Fianna Fáil, built on its
superior grass–roots organisation and socio–economic policies with
widespread support among the urban working class, marginalised
the Labour Party. At the same time, the economic strategy of self-
sufficiency won Fianna Fáil support from the business community
and from farmers at the expense of Cumann na nGaedheal.

Farmers' parties did emerge in Ireland in the 1920s and 1940s.
One, the Farmers' Party, an example of an interest group-
sponsored party as the political vehicle of the Irish Farmers'
Union, was for a time a relatively successful minor party. But
though their support was crucial for some governments, they
never made the necessary electoral breakthrough. Like other
minor parties which appealed to a section of the electorate,
farmers' parties were short–lived. Successful minor party TDs
(members of the Dáil) often ended up joining one of the two major
groups.

Formation of Fine Gael

In 1933 the National Centre Party, Cumann na nGaedheal, and the National Guard merged to form Fine Gael. The National Guard, commonly known as the Blueshirts, had been formed as an unofficial defence force for Cumann na nGaedheal. Its leader, General Eoin O'Duffy, the former Commissioner of Police, became the president of Fine Gael. O'Duffy's semi-fascist beliefs were an embarrassment to the party and he was replaced by William T. Cosgrave, the former leader of Cumann na nGaedheal. Fine Gael is still sometimes taunted by its opponents with the tags 'Blueshirts' or 'right-wing' but the party contains much the same ideological spectrum as Fianna Fáil. Both main parties refuse to define themselves as of the political left or of the right. They claim to represent all classes and creeds.

Coalition politics

The development of Fianna Fáil into a catch-all party made an anti-Fianna Fáil coalition difficult to achieve. It was not until 1948 that coalitions became practical. The coalitions or, as they were known, 'inter-party governments', of 1948–51 and 1954–57, involved parties whose policies, particularly on socio-economic issues, were very diverse. Dissimilar parties were driven together by the dominance of Fianna Fáil. Without coalitions, parties other than Fianna Fáil would not have been able to serve in government.

The major reason why Fianna Fáil's predominance was challenged in the 1950s was the fact that the economy began to experience severe difficulties. Some politicians in all parties argued for a change in economic strategy, but it was Fianna Fáil which developed a new economic direction. It decided to open up the Irish economy to foreign trade. Tariffs and quotas on Irish exports would be removed and incentives provided to foreign firms to set up in Ireland. Fianna Fáil activated this open trade policy when it was returned to office in 1957.

The change in economic policy induced economic growth in Ireland. This led to reductions in both unemployment and emigration. At the same time living standards increased. The economic prosperity won Fianna Fáil electoral support and reinforced its position as a 'catch-all' party. It enabled it to win four consecutive general elections and remain in office for another sixteen-year period. Under this second era of extended Fianna Fáil rule, there were several developments in the party system. Firstly, the 1960s saw a decrease in the number of parties. In 1961 seven different parties sat in the Dáil along with six independents. By 1969 only the three major parties had seats, along with one independent. Secondly, the two opposition groups had become disillusioned with the coalition strategy. They both found the previous coalitions unsatisfactory, particularly that of 1954–57. Also, both Fine Gael and Labour believed through the early 1960s that they were on the verge of making an electoral breakthrough. The failure of either Fine Gael or Labour to make any significant headway in 1969 brought the question of coalition back on to the agenda. Fine Gael made only slight improvements in its votes and seats, while Labour actually lost ground. Both parties realised that without coalition neither could hope to take office. For the general election in 1973, a coalition strategy was agreed.

Fighting an election as a coalition can be of great value because of the Irish electoral system. This is proportional representation by the single transferable vote in multi-member constituencies. Each constituency returns between three and five TDs. The elector can vote for all the candidates, listing them in order of preference. A quota is worked out by the following formula:

$$\frac{\text{Total valid poll}}{\text{No. of seats} + 1} + 1$$

When a candidate reaches the quota he or she is elected and the surplus of votes is allocated to the other candidates according to the preferences on the ballot paper. Thus, if two parties have a coalition pact before an election they can ask their supporters to give their second preference vote to the other partner.

The benefits of a pre-election pact were clear after the 1973 general election. Although Fianna Fáil increased its vote slightly, it lost six seats. Fine Gael also increased its vote slightly but gained four seats. Labour dropped by 3 per cent in the poll. Nevertheless, the coalition won an extra five seats over their combined total in 1969 because of the transfer of votes between them.

In the run-up to the general election in 1977 the coalition partners failed to note the ominous signs against them. After the 1973 defeat Fianna Fáil had overhauled its organisation and had set out to capture the 'youth vote'. This section of the population is extremely important, because around 50 per cent of Irish people and, therefore, a significant part of the electorate, are under twenty-five. Fianna Fáil appealed to the voters with a combination of tax reductions and new jobs. It won eighty-four seats, an increase of sixteen seats over the 1973 total, while Fine Gael lost eleven and Labour three. For only the second time a party had won over 50 per cent of the vote.

With the impressive position of Fianna Fáil in 1977, it might have been expected it was embarking on another long spell in office. But this was not to be the case. The major reason for the decline in the party's popularity was its inability to deliver its promises. In face of increased tension in the north, Charles Haughey, who replaced Jack Lynch as party leader and Taoiseach in 1979, singled out the unification of the country as the single most important issue in the election campaign of 1981. Fine Gael concentrated on the economy and won more seats and votes than ever before. In the new Dáil, Fine Gael had sixty-five seats, Fianna Fáil seventy-eight and Labour fifteen. The coalition partners agreed on a joint programme and formed a government while Fianna Fáil became the opposition. The coalition, which depended on the tacit support of some independents, lasted until February 1982.

The February 1982 election changed the government, but only briefly. Fianna Fáil gained three seats, making the number up to eighty-one, and formed the government with the support of an independent and the small Workers' Party. The new administration was only able to stay in office until November 1982. After swingeing cuts in social services, the Workers' Party felt unable to support it further and the government was defeated in the Dáil. At the ensuing general election Fianna Fáil lost six seats, Fine Gael gained seven and Labour one. This gave Fine Gael and Labour a combined overall majority. Labour entered coalition once again.

The 'new right'

The failure of Fianna Fáil to regain its traditional position as the 'natural' governing party of the Republic precipitated a challenge to the leadership of Charles Haughey. Opposition to the party leader was based on his style of leadership, his stance on Northern Ireland, and his conservative views on moral issues such as divorce. There were also reservations about his attitude to the economy. He favoured increased spending to promote growth and job creation while others in the party wanted more controls on expenditure. The main challenger to Haughey was Desmond O'Malley. Eventually O'Malley formed the Progressive Demo-crats (PDs), and several Fianna Fáil TDs joined him. The PDs are clearly on the political 'right', in the mould of classic European liberals but, in Irish terms, are radical on certain social issues. The emergence of such a party may be a sign of further developments in the party system.

The main theme dominating the Dáil after 1982 was the state of the economy. The coalition attempted to reduce Ireland's foreign borrowing, without success. Although it managed to cut the inflation rate dramatically, unemployment soared and with it emigration. In January 1987 Fine Gael introduced a budget involving widespread cutbacks in government expenditure. The Labour deputies were unable to support the reductions in welfare rates so they resigned and provoked a general election. Fine Gael fought the election on its austerity budget. The PDs adopted the economic strategy of the 'new right'. This includes decreasing substantially government involvement in the economy, privatisa-tion, decreased spending on welfare provision and large tax cuts. Fianna Fáil, while accepting that 90 per cent of the Fine Gael budget would have to be introduced, committed itself to investing in targeted areas to increase economic growth, to creating jobs and maintaining welfare benefits. Labour said that welfare benefits would have to be maintained and the tax net widened to increase the contribution made by farmers and the self-employed.

The outcome of the 1987 election was a minority Fianna Fáil government. An examination of the results, however, reveals some cause for concern for Ireland's dominant party. While Fianna Fáil voters transferred their preferences overwhelmingly to candidates within the party, these candidates received relatively few transfers from outside. Further, the Progressive Democrats made some significant inroads on Fianna Fáil, especially where former party members stood. Perhaps most significant for the future of the Irish party system was a trend for Fianna Fáil to lose support among the middle classes. Overall Fianna Fáil achieved its lowest share of the vote in twenty-six years, Fine Gael in thirty years and Labour in fifty-four years. In contrast, the PDs made the most dramatic debut for a new party in forty years.

The minority opposition of the government was eased considerably by the decision of Fine Gael to give conditional support for its central policies. The main parties agreed on the need for sharp reductions in public spending and reduced government borrowing. Though it was defeated five times in the Dáil, the government lost no crucial vote. Nevertheless, the Taoiseach, Mr Haughey, called a general election in June 1989. Opinion polls had been indicating that the government might win an overall majority. In the event, Fianna Fáil lost seats despite securing 44 per cent of first preference votes, as in 1987. Its performance only served to emphasise Fianna Fáil's dependence on other parties. Fine Gael and the PDs had entered an agreement on coalition during the election campaign. The PDs, however, lost heavily and, though Fine Gael did improve by four seats, the parties' combined total of sixty-one was well short of the eighty-four needed for a Dáil majority. The left-wing parties, Labour and the Workers' Party, fared better but ruled out any participation in government. Ireland was thus faced with several weeks of uncertainty before a coalition government involving Fianna Fáil and the Progressive Democrats was formed in mid-July.

The major question for Irish politics of the 1989 election again concerns the future role of Fianna Fáil. Since its foundation in 1926 the party has provided the single-party government on fourteen of nineteen possible occasions following general elections. Fianna Fáil had eschewed coalitions and represented itself as 'the national party'. It had, however, failed to maintain its hegemony. It looks likely that for the foreseeable future Fianna Fáil will only be able to rule by sharing power. The party's dominance of Irish politics received a further blow in November 1990 when the left-wing independent, Mary Robinson, won the first presidential election since 1973. She had a comfortable victory, after the second count, over Fianna Fáil's Brian Lenihan and Fine Gael's Austin Currie.

Ms Robinson was the candidate backed by the Labour Party with the support of the Workers' Party and other left-wing groupings. The Progressive Democrats did not formally recommend any candidate but several prominent members spoke glowingly about Robinson. Ms Robinson had been a member of Seanad Eireann and was closely associated with several liberal causes. During her campaign she rejected the description 'socialist' though her past support for socialism was referred to frequently by her opponents.

For the left wing of Irish politics, Robinson's poll was taken as a sign that an attractively and sensitively presented campaign can bring electoral success. In Fine Gael, the reverberations of their defeat were felt almost immediately. Alan Dukes, facing the prospect of a vote of no confidence from the Fine Gael parliamentary party, resigned as leader to be replaced by John Bruton. Though Fianna Fáil's vote in the Presidential election was the same as in the previous general election, the 1990 result represented a major disappointment. The presidential election was the sixth occasion under Charles Haughey at which it had failed to win a national contest and many party supporters questioned the leadership approach to coalition with the Progressive Democrats, party organisation and the presidential campaign.

Class politics?

It may be that Ireland is developing a class-based party system similar to other European countries. If so the Progressive Democrats, who made such a spectacular showing at their first general election, may emerge as the party of the middle class. The PDs performance in 1989, however, indicates that they will have to compete with Fine Gael for that section of the electorate. It is possible that some understanding on transferring preference votes and post-election agreements may see these two parties come to a long-term pact.

The 1989 election showed again that Fianna Fáil is increasingly a party of the middle class. Its traditional working-class support is being eroded, though Fianna Fáil still remains the strongest single party among all classes. The main competitors for the votes of the working class are the Labour and Workers' Parties. The Labour Party's claim to be the major left-wing force in the Republic was enhanced by its much increased vote in 1989. It also gained considerably from the successful campaign of Mary Robinson, in which it took a leading role. Labour's strategy, however, is to increase its distinctive left-wing appeal by avoiding coalitions with what it characterises as right-wing parties, including Fianna Fáil. It is clear that there will be no more Fine Gael–Labour arrangements before or after a general election for a long time.

For the moment, Ireland looks like retaining its distinctive party system, with two large 'catch-all' parties and a varying number of smaller parties. The Progressive Democrats may establish themselves as a permanent force, unlike the numerous other parties which have come and gone quickly. In the long run, however, it is difficult in such a small and socially homogeneous country to oust the established parties. The conservative economic outlook of the landowning Irish farm family, the smallness of the urban proletariat, the importance of the symbols of national unity, the broad consensus on social values and the slow pace of economic restructuring militate against radical changes in the party system.

The style of political competition

The stability of the party system, the lack of deep ideological divisions between the main parties and a tradition of strict party discipline in the Oireachtas have had an important effect on the way individual politicians compete for election. Irish electors generally remain faithful to one political party. Elections are won or lost by relatively few voters switching their support and by parties' success in persuading their supporters to cast their votes. Even when new parties emerge, their success is often short-lived.

Under the Irish system of proportional representation, in multi-member constituencies, individual politicians must compete not only against the candidates of other parties, but also fellow party nominees. Fianna Fáil or Fine Gael may win or lose but the main priority for each politician is that he or she is personally successful. To ensure success regardless of party fortunes a politician must have some basis of support among the electorate other than partisan allegiance. Politicians of earlier generations could often rely on being supported because of their role in the struggle for independence or their stand during the Civil War. Today no candidate can be so assured. Clearly the parties do not permit open displays of disagreement at election time so candidates of the same party cannot compete for support on the basis of policy. Irish politicians, therefore, emphasise their social, local and personal links with the electorate. In Chapter 3, the importance of social and local connections to the politician's career is examined.

Personal support is generally based on the exchange of favours, or the illusion of a favour. Most Irish people believe that public authorities are best approached by some intermediary or influential person. The basis for this belief may well lie in the centuries of domination by a colonial power, but it persists long after independence. Thus, people are not identified primarily in their formal roles as lawyers, businessmen, councillors, ministers, etc., but in the first place as friends or friends of friends, relatives of friends or people with whom there is some close contact or reciprocal basis for a favour. The use of such contacts and the calling-in of such favours is considered legitimate on both sides, by those with the authority and influence as well as by those seeking to use the same. The need for local intermediaries is reinforced by the relatively low level of subjective civic competence. It has had the effect of producing politicians who are primarily brokers rather than legislators. A great deal of an Irish politician's time is taken up telephoning or writing to government ministers, civil servants, local government managers and others in authority on behalf of constituents.

Politicians try to gather sufficient personal support to be elected ahead of their party colleagues. Each candidate will ask for a first preference vote for him or herself and subsequent votes for fellow party nominees. The greatest rivalries in Irish politics are often within parties rather than between them. A substantial personal following insulates the sitting TD from the effects of his party's occasional unpopularity and for some deputies, such as the leading PDs, it may facilitate election after a change of party. Irish and foreign commentators frequently forecast the demise of brokerage in the face of increased education, wealth and sophistication. Nevertheless, the system remains important.

Conclusion

The party system in Ireland is different from most European party systems because it is not based as much on social cleavages. This is because social cleavages were relatively weak at the formation of the party system. The major issue after independence in 1922 was the Anglo-Irish Treaty. The division this produced formed the basis of the Irish party system. This issue has, however, subsided since the 1930s. The success of Irish parties now depends on their economic appeal to the electorate in general and the loyalty of their traditional supporters.

Alternative solutions to economic problems have long been the mainstay of Irish general election campaigns. Fianna Fáil's predominance in the electoral system owes much to its ability to advance the economic prosperity of the country. It did this from 1932 to 1948 with its policy of economic self-sufficiency. When this strategy reached the limits of its usefulness, the electorate began to look to other parties and vote against the incumbent government. In the four consecutive general elections of 1948, 1951, 1954 and 1957, governments were voted out of office.

The Fianna Fáil government of 1957 developed a new economic strategy, based on industrialisation through inviting foreign firms into the country. The economic prosperity which resulted enabled it to win a further three general elections. The general election of 1973 ended Fianna Fáil's second run of sixteen years in office. It also ushered in a new period of uncertainty in Irish politics.

Since the beginning of the 1970s Ireland has been faced with growing inflation, unemployment and national debt. Once more the electorate has tended to vote against governments. In the seven general elections from 1969 to 1987, the government has lost office each time. In 1989, though it retained its share of the vote, a Fianna Fail government was forced into a coalition for the first time, having been denied a clear majority. The major question about the Irish party system which is still to be resolved is whether the major partisan division, based on the Sinn Féin split over the 1922 Treaty, will give way to one reflecting more explicit class or economic divisions in Irish society.

Further reading

M. Gallagher, *Political Parties in the Republic of Ireland*, Manchester: Manchester University Press, 1985.

M. Gallagher & R. Sinnot (eds.), *How Ireland Voted, 1989*, Galway: PSAI Press, 1990.

P. Mair, *The Changing Irish Party System*, London: Frances Pinter, 1987.

3

ELITES AND PRESSURE GROUPS

Power in Ireland is organised into a range of private and public institutions such as large companies, banks, government departments, state-sponsored enterprises and major pressure groups. The nation's private wealth is concentrated in relatively few hands and control of public resources is also dominated by a small number of individuals. Such a distribution of power is usual in liberal democratic capitalist societies. In this chapter we will examine the nature of the elites and the influence of the main pressure groups. Following Parry, we will take elites to be 'small minorities who appear to play an exceptionally influential part in political and social affairs'[1]

Studies of countries much larger than Ireland have shown remarkable levels of concentration of power. Some social theorists – notably Weber and Durkheim – have sought to show that as societies develop, individual functions within them become more specialised. To such theorists, the cohesion of the social structure demands co-ordinating elites. Ironically, as more avenues for individual advancement are opened up and people are freed from social traditions, so specialised power roles are created. Some level of elite co-ordination appears essential for social stability, even in democracies.

In Ireland the number of people in key positions of private and institutional power is small enough for elite members to be known and accessible to each other. Members of the Irish elites may have ascended from different professional paths but there are often common elements in their educational and social backgrounds.

Similarly, some points of convergence can be shown in terms of political and social attitudes. In general terms, the various elites accept the economic values of capitalist development based on profit-making and they reject other forms of development. The advantages of private property are recognised as justified and a degree of active social inequality seen as functional. The political and administrative elites' outlook on development through the encouragement and defence of manufacturing, trading and agricultural business enterprise coincides with that of the economic elite.

In this chapter we will examine the Irish elites by looking at those people who, by occupying positions of influence and control in major institutions, can be described as 'powerful'. It is assumed that once they are in such elite positions their power is felt by society in general whether they act consciously to influence particular decisions or not.

The economic elite

The economic elite is taken to be individuals who own substantial amounts of productive property or who occupy top positions in the most important firms. In Ireland, it has been estimated that 1 per cent of the population owns around a third of the wealth and 5 per cent account for nearly two-thirds. Recent reports put the number who are poor at nearly one-third. These figures have been challenged on points of detail but the general pattern of inequality is clear. Personal wealth in itself is not a measure of power except when it is associated with high institutional status. Some wealthy people may make no direct impact on society at large. It is not clear whether Ireland's wealthiest citizens are also part of the managerial elite that now dominates large corporations, banks and other financial institutions. It is clear, however, that access to political or administrative elite positions is not notably easier for the particularly wealthy. As will be shown below, Irish civil servants and members of the Oireachtas are not marked out by the same social distance from the population they serve as in countries such as Britain.

Many of Ireland's wealthiest citizens retain their wealth in the form of agricultural property. On the whole, however, the pattern of landholding is relatively static. Only 2,319 of Ireland's 263,558 agricultural holdings are above 300 acres. The great majority of farms are owned and operated by the same family from generation to generation. The land reforms of the late nineteenth century reduced considerably the number and influence of large land-owners. Only one Irish public company, the Smurfit Group, is in the 'Fortune 500' – a list of the world's largest capitalist enterprises. Smurfit is 498th, but in Irish terms it is very large. In line with several of the biggest Irish businesses and banks, the Smurfit Group has diversified abroad. Irish business executives have been given increased prominence in recent years and some, such as the supermarket-chain owner, Feargal Quinn, have been active in the public domain. The chief executives of the biggest agricultural co-operatives and other related businesses have become influential members of the economic elite. Many of the firms with the largest turnovers, however, are owned by foreigners.

In manufacturing industry, one-third of the work-force is employed by foreign-owned firms and many Irish factories are really 'dependent' upon foreign management decisions. Such foreign firms are most dominant in the larger and expanding industrial projects so that their economic influence is even greater. The proportion of senior managerial staff in such Irish-based foreign enterprises is small and the major managerial, professional and research functions are unlikely to be carried out in Ireland.

Irish influence in manufacturing mainly comes via the state, which by facilitating both foreign and domestic investment, as well as investing directly, is at the centre of industrial activity. The state bureaucracy at the higher levels sees itself as being in the same 'enterprise' as private managers and in partnership with state sponsored companies. Thus the answer to the question 'Who is in the economic elite?', in the sense of who occupies key institutional positions of power, revolves around the identity of senior bureaucrats as well as managers.

Research on the economic elite is very sparse and many everyday assertions about it are little more than speculation. It is apparent, however, that the economic elite is relatively stable and exercises some 'control' over its own membership. Clearly, the privately wealthy may retain their advantage through the working of inheritance, good accountants and a relatively favourable tax regime for wealth as distinct from income. Those of managerial and higher professional status are also restricted by social opportunities as well as ability. The intragenerational stability of social groupings in Ireland is remarkable. In a study of Dublin, Whelan and Whelan examined the composition of what they call 'the elite classes':

Thirty-five per cent of the men currently in this higher class are themselves sons of higher professional and managerial fathers; a further 40 per cent are drawn from the other white collar classes and the petty bourgeoisie. Thus, 75 per cent of the occupants of higher professional and managerial classes are drawn from just four classes; the corresponding figure for England and Wales is 47 per cent. Similarly, only 14 per cent of higher professional and managerial respondents had working-class origins, a figure which is half the corresponding one for England and Wales.[2]

Put in another way, the chances of a man born into the highest social bracket staying in that group are 240 times greater than of someone born in the lower classes rising to the top. These figures are of course too global to apply directly to the elites looked at here. Nevertheless, the background to our study of elites is one of high social stability.

Further, in Ireland, a person's first occupation, which is heavily influenced by early educational attainment, has an extremely significant effect on where in the economic hierarchy he or she is currently employed. In effect, not many people who start in manual and semi-skilled jobs gain professional or managerial posts later in life. Part of the explanation for this social rigidity is that despite the increased availability of free post-primary education, participation rates in higher education are many times greater for the offspring of professionals and managers than other social categories. In addition, some of the children of the economic elite attend fee-paying secondary schools which offer both educational and social advantages.

With independence, and to a large degree before it, the upper or 'ascendancy' class that was associated with the British regime became socially marginalised. The social elite of the new state was decidedly bourgeois, dominated by the mercantile and shopkeeping classes. Historically the Irish bourgeoisie was based essentially on trade. Throughout the eighteenth century, Catholics were prevented from owning land, except on relatively short leases. Catholics were also excluded from public office. They thus directed their wealth and energy into trade – a large proportion of economic activity, especially for an island. Much of the profit earned from this business was invested abroad and in commercial rather than manufacturing ventures. One of the main arguments for relaxing the 'penal laws', as the anti-Catholic legislation was known, was that this would encourage the wealth held by Catholics to be invested in the country and, thereby, increase economic activity in Ireland. As the laws were abolished, however, towards the end of the eighteenth century, the Catholic bourgeoisie did not put the bulk of their money into industrial development as was hoped. They had little experience in industrial matters. Further, there was greater uncertainty in industrial projects in Ireland because of British competition.

At independence, the more prosperous Irish were in trade, farming or the professions. Where they were involved in industry it tended to be on a small scale. Social mobility for the smaller farmers and tradespeople often involved entry to the traditional professions, which were highly regarded in terms of status and security. For these groups, it is the large bureaucracies like the civil service, local government and public administration which provide the main channel for upward mobility into the professional and managerial class.

Political elites

The personalised nature of Irish electoral competition encourages a wide interest in the details of politicians' private lives. For this reason directories of national and local politicians are more widely read in Ireland than elsewhere. The most obvious characteristic of deputies, senators and councillors is that the proportion of men is much higher than in the electorate. In this respect Irish politicians, particularly deputies, are not dissimilar to those in all European legislatures.

Other characteristics of politicians in Western democracies are also displayed in Ireland: deputies are disproportionately drawn from the liberal professions, especially teaching and law; and they are twice as likely to have completed a secondary education and over three times as likely to have a degree as the general population. Although farmers are very much in evidence in the Dáil, they are nevertheless under-represented in terms of their numbers in the country. The dominance of the professions is even more marked at ministerial level: almost 60 per cent of ministers since 1922 have come from this group. Businessmen are also well represented among ministers, although in some cases it is hard to know with what size of enterprises they have links.

The professional background and educational attainment of politicians do not tell us anything about their views or policy preferences. To assume, for example, that better-off individuals are less sensitive to the plight of the poor may be misleading. What the evidence does tell us is that certain groups such as manual workers, women and the socially disadvantaged generally do not make it to the top as politicians.

As we saw in Chapter 2, it is important for a candidate at an Irish election to become known personally to the electorate. This process is, of course, eased if your 'name' is already established. Twenty-six per cent of deputies are related to former members; indeed, often they are their sons. 'Heredity', therefore, plays an important part in elite selection. Other forms of ready identification such as sporting repute may also help an individual aspiring to the political elite; 15 per cent of incumbents in the 1980s were prominent in sport.

The route to the national political elite commonly involves service in local government. Almost 80 per cent of TDs have been councillors. Again, local services help a would-be deputy establish his or her name in the potential Dáil constituency. A local government track record may be particularly important for a candidate without the social advantages of professional status or educational attainment.

Local government service, local family connections and local prestige are the most important qualifications for entry to the political elite. That elite is not notable for any great social distance from the electorate, though lower status occupations are clearly at a marked disadvantage. Oireachtas membership changes only slowly, despite the competitive rhetoric of elections. Once elected, a deputy or, to a lesser extent, a senator can expect a reasonably long career. Often, membership of the Seanad is used to introduce new members or protect electorally defeated members of the political elite and this adds to the group's stability. Though they are bound to emphasise partisan differences, and subtly establish their own 'personal' images, Irish politicians share many interests and values. Among these are loyalty to parliamentary democracy, nationalism, the moral ethos of the Catholic Church and a belief that politicians collectively make a worthwhile contribution to the nation. Further, like most stable groups, the political elite constitutes a fairly cohesive informal social network reflecting common patterns of work, income and leisure.

Administrative elites

The political elite, as defined above, includes all members of the Oireachtas. This is almost certainly too broad if the criteria for inclusion featured direct and sustained influence on policy. One group, however, represents an established centre of power. After independence, the Free State bureaucracy became as central an institution as its British predecessor. The enormous importance of the civil service and, to a lesser extent, the state-sponsored bureaucracies was heightened by the dominance of the public sector in the rather underdeveloped economy of the post-independence period. Because of its political indispensability, the civil service was able to retain its corporate integrity and identity and resist pressures towards politicisation. The result of this situation was the creation and survival of a 'powerful bureaucracy', independent of the party machine.

Here we will look primarily at the higher civil servants, those at principal level and above. In 1984, 392 people were in such positions. These posts are recognised as crucial because their occupants control vital information and supply advice to the senior political leaders. As we will see in Chapter 4, higher civil servants often make important policy decisions independently of politicians and they certainly shape policy significantly. Of course, senior politicians do have sources of advice outside the civil service but in Ireland, more than in most democracies, power is highly centralised in the state bureaucracy. The most senior public servants at local government level are the county or city managers; this group is, therefore, briefly examined here also.

The recruitment and promotion procedures of the Irish public service, local and national, are formally and rigorously meritocratic. The central tenet of the merit principle is that persons selected for posts in the public service have the requisite skill and knowledge. Though public service recruitment is controversial elsewhere, particularly in newly-independent states, in Ireland there has been no sustained challenge to a system based on qualifications. It is assumed such an arrangement removes the dangers of inefficiency and favouritism associated with political appointment. In fact, civil servants and local government officers are recruited by the Civil Service and the Local Appointments Commissions respectively, the political neutrality and absolute independence of which are in no doubt.

Most civil servants (other than those in special technical grades) joined the public service at junior levels straight from school, though the proportion of graduate entrants is increasing. A similar trend towards graduate entry may occur at local government level now that some middle-rank posts have been opened up to graduates. The normal model for incumbent high-level public servants has been junior entry followed by in-service training, third-level education, through evening classes and day-release, and a steady progress up the ranks via examinations and competitive interviews. The Departments of Finance and Foreign Affairs are exceptions in that most of its senior people enter the service as graduates.

The higher civil servants have their critics, but few can doubt their qualities of industry and ambition. Indeed most criticisms have centred on the presumed dulling effects of such sustained practical and diligent work in a hierarchical organisation. The civil service is accused of being too unimaginative, insulated from ideas in the outside world and disproportionately concerned with short-term objectives. This narrowness of outlook is reinforced by the absence in Ireland of any significant movement between private and public employment.

The general pattern of promotion, particularly at higher levels, has been for civil servants to rise within one department. Though in recent years, there has been greater mobility between departments in filling top posts, many higher civil servants have come to accept a particular approach to their department's area of specialism. This 'departmental line' is obviously tempered by the current political realities, but it may represent an underlying theme in civil service advice. It is obviously difficult to work in a particular area of policy for a significant proportion of a career and not develop some firm views on that policy. Common ideas do provide a certain internal cohesion to the group. To a lesser degree, a communality of outlook has developed throughout the administrative elite which rests on a sense of its own indispensability, corporate responsibility and self-interest.

The administrative elite work in a system, the main organisational characteristics of which were inherited from Britain. In Ireland, however, the elite is not marked out by social distance from other public servants. There is no tradition, as in Britain, of social exclusivity. The main barrier to entry into the public service is educational achievement, which in Ireland has been facilitated for almost all classes by free or inexpensive secondary schooling. There is a tendency for higher civil servants to have attended schools run by priests, brothers or nuns, because such religious have been to the forefront in providing secondary education down through the years; but there is no 'old school tie' tradition.

The number of women at the principal officer or counsellor level, though small, is growing, as is the number at assistant principal. In 1982, 26 per cent of assistant principals, the grade below principal rank, were women. This is over six times the number in 1972. At local government level, none of the managerial posts has ever been held by a woman.

The administrative elite is not marked out educationally, culturally or socially from other Irish elites. The senior civil servant is particularly powerful, however. He operates at the core of the highly centralised, secretive, self-protective, pervasive and unrivalled administrative machine outlined in Chapter 4. None of the other elites can bring the same level of sustained, informed and rigorous attention to any public issue as the administrative elite.

The local government managers are also powerful but are less shielded from public criticism because they are publicly accountable for their actions and advice. The managers are also further from the legislative processes and in a figurative and literal sense, too distant from Dublin. They do have a degree of autonomy from their politicians and are clearly at the hub of the local administration. But local government itself is too subject to central control to provide a sustainable basis for rivalling the higher civil servants. In the health service, the equivalents of the managers, while they administer major services, are even more clearly subordinate to Dublin. Socially and educationally they are from similar backgrounds to civil servants. They have, however, typically worked in several parts of the country.

Major interest groups

One of the important common features of the Irish elite discussed above is a high level of self-conscious nationalism. This attitude is a product both of Ireland's comparatively recent independent status and its proximity to a much more powerful and older state. In part this rationalism is expressed in terms of the support given to the Irish language as a symbol of identity and separateness. More importantly, however, it is reflected in elites' positive attitudes to economic development and relative lack of concern about environmental and social disruption. The elites' outlook on development gives the representatives of economic interest groups an important 'insider' status in the formulation of public policy. It also fashions the terms of public discussion and gives an advantage to those that can present their private interests as congruent to the national interest.

The major economic interest groups are portrayed as 'partners' with government and their participation in policy formulation is formalised in numerous advisory and consultative bodies such as the National Economic and Social Council (NESC). In October 1987 the 'social partners' arrived at an agreement, the 'Programme for National Recovery', covering pay rises and social benefits for three years. The Programme is evidence of the so called 'corporatist' style of policy-making in Ireland, as were its predecessors, the 'National Agreements' and 'National Understandings'. The main difference between the Programme and previous arrangements is that it involves the agricultural sector as well as the government, business and unions. Similarly, three-year targets were set in 1991 by the Programme for Economic and Social Progress as part of a longer ten-year strategy involving the 'social partners'.

The two main groups representing employers' interests are the Confederation of Irish Industry (CII) and the Federated Union of Employers (FUE). The CII exerts pressure both through lobbying ministers and publicity in the press, radio and television. Its main arguments are that the creation of new jobs, a national priority, will only be accomplished by expansion of the industrial sector; but the restricted national market does not allow this expansion which depends heavily upon the success of exports. It is necessary, therefore, to create an environment favourable to exporting products by enhancing their competitiveness. The CII is primarily concerned with macro-economic issues.

The FUE is the more important of the two employers' bodies. It represents affiliated companies in negotiations with government and the unions, particularly in agreements such as the Programme for National Recovery. The FUE is financed by subscriptions from member companies. It provides a pension-planning service and legal advice on occupational health and safety and labour relations. It represents members at the Labour Court, the Employment Appeal Tribunal, Equality Officer Hearings before a Rights Commissioner and other arbitration proceedings. The

FUE organises members' conferences and it keeps them up to date on developments in member companies in relation to pay and working conditions. The FUE also has a European Affairs Unit and helps to maintain the Irish Business Bureau in Brussels.

The trade unions

The struggle for independence in Ireland left an indelible mark on the trade unions on the island for several decades after the Irish Free State was established. The radical leadership of James Connolly, James Larkin and others in the second decade of this century saw a major role for the labour movement in the fight for self-government. Connolly's vision went beyond the purely nationalist struggle. He argued that freedom from Britain was only a part of the greater struggle for freedom from the capitalist system. As Connolly put it: 'If you remove the English army tomorrow and hoist the green flag over Dublin Castle, unless you set about the organisation of the Socialist Republic your efforts would be in vain!'[3] Following the defeat of the unions in the 1913 Dublin lock-out, Larkin went to America and did not return until after independence.

In 1916 Connolly was executed for his part in the Easter Rising. The new leaders of labour had a more restricted view of the political role of workers in the developing independence struggle. Partition in 1922 was a major problem for the unions. They were organised on an all-Ireland basis. Many were British-based. After independence, many workers in the Free State wanted to have Irish-based unions, while the Unionist workers in the Northern State resented any tendency which would lead to the Trade Union Congress (TUC) becoming dominated by nationalists. New unions based in the Free State grew in the 1920s and 1930s and by the mid-1930s they accounted for almost half of the affiliated membership of the Irish TUC. In 1944 eighteen of the Irish based unions split off from the TUC and formed the Irish Congress of Trade Unions (ICTU).

The ICTU today has eighty-six affiliated trade unions, representing over 672,000 workers. Of the members in unions affiliated to the ICTU, 446,000 are in the Republic (approximately sixty-one unions) and 226,000 in Northern Ireland (approximately forty-three unions). There are eighteen unions with members in both the Republic and Northern Ireland. The three largest unions until recently were the Irish Transport and General Workers' Union (ITGWU), the Amalgamated Transport and General Workers' Union (ATGWU) and the Federated Workers' Union of Ireland (FWUI) which account for around 40 per cent of union members. Unions not affiliated to the ICTU represent around 10 per cent of unionised workers. Union membership as a proportion of people in work is relatively stable but some unions have merged to ensure they retain sufficient membership. In 1990 the ITGWU and the FWUI joined forces to form the Services, Industry, Professional, Technical Union (SIPTU), which has over 200,000 members. Similarly, the bodies representing many local government and civil service employees are now merged in IMPACT with a membership of around 35,000. In order to avoid a possible split, the ICTU takes no formal position on partition. It also tends to be non-partisan in the party politics of the Republic. The ICTU is aware that Fianna Fáil has always attracted more of the working-class vote than the Labour Party.

The primary concern of the trade unions in Ireland, as in other liberal democratic countries, is the protection and improvement of workers' working conditions and pay. Between 1970 and 1982 they did this within the National Wage Agreement (NWA) structure. The NWAs were tripartite agreements, made between government, employers and unions, on pay settlements throughout the economy. The union saw the NWAs as the means of maintaining, if not improving, workers' conditions at a time of increasing economic difficulty. In the tripartite negotiations, the unions made some useful manoeuvres which strengthened their negotiating position. From the mid-1970s they delayed agreements until they were able to put demands to government on what they wanted included in the Budget. The greatest successes the unions had in NWAs were in the years 1979 and 1980. The economy was going through difficulties and the Fianna Fáil government needed industrial peace. It was, therefore, willing to extend the agreements on wages to other issues such as job creation, taxation of the farming community and improvements in social welfare. The coalition of 1982 abandoned the tripartite machinery but the subsequent Fianna Fáil government revived it in a series of National Understandings. The National Understandings covered social benefits as well as pay and can be seen as the precursor of the 1987 Programme for National Recovery (PNR). The PNR includes government commitments on job creation and tax equity which the ICTU sought.

The farmers

Land has traditionally held an important position for Irish people. Up until the 1930s it was seen as the life-blood of the economy. Today it still makes a major contribution to the wealth of the country. But land, and the people who work it, have long been regarded as much more than economic assets. The ownership of land is charged with much social, political and cultural significance. The model of the family farm remains an important part of Ireland's self-image. The transfer of ownership effected in the late nineteenth century means that at present more than 90 per cent of Irish farmers own their land.

One of the two largest farming organisations, the Irish Creamery Milk Suppliers' Association (ICMSA) was founded in 1950 to campaign on behalf of farmers who produced milk. The bulk of milk production used to come from small farms. This pattern has changed and now 12 per cent of suppliers provide 40 per cent of the milk sent to creameries. The number of milk suppliers has reduced in recent years and now stands at about 58,000. The ICMSA has, therefore, had to broaden its appeal. The ICMSA was a militant organisation and in 1953 called a strike to support its demand for an increase in the price paid to farmers for their milk. The strike ended after sixteen days when the increase was granted. But for some years after the strike, the ICMSA came to be regarded as fairly conservative. Recently, however, it has been involved in street protests on the issue of tax reform. The ICMSA believes in intensification of agricultural

production on small farms. It is suspicious of land reform and
European Community programmes for modernisation and the
retirement of elderly farmers. The ICMSA has its headquarters in
Limerick and organises its 52,000 members through 480 branches
throughout the country. The main farming organisation, however,
is the Irish Farmers' Association (IFA). The IFA grew out of the
National Farmers' Association (NFA), which was set up in 1955.
It developed into a highly efficient organisation and employs
agricultural experts to present its case to government for improvements in farming. With a membership of over 150,000, the
IFA is regarded by many as Ireland's most effective interest
group. Even before Ireland joined, the IFA realised the importance of the EC and opened an office in Brussels. Unlike the
ICMSA, the IFA believes in increasing production in farming in
response to market conditions. By the mid-1960s the IFA was
recognised by government as the farmers' representative to be
consulted regularly on the formulation of agricultural policy. The
IFA was very militant in the 1960s, reflecting farmers' anger at
their economic difficulties. There was the feeling amongst the
farming community that it had been left behind in the economic
plan which concentrated on the development of an Irish industrial
sector. During the militant campaigns of the 1960s, farmers went
to gaol as a result of protests. Today, the IFA is far more
integrated into the national policy-making system. In contrast to
the ICMSA, the IFA signed the PNR in 1987. The greatest
overall improvement for Irish agriculture came with entry to the
EC. As well as bringing higher and guaranteed prices, the
Community has attempted to modernise farming, by encouraging
the enlargement of farms, the use of better technology and the
education of farmers. Though the number of small farms, i.e.
under thirty acres has declined, the rate has been much slower
than many expected.

The Catholic Church

One force in Ireland which has had, and still has, a major
influence on Irish society is the Catholic Church. In 1911, almost

90 per cent of the population of the twenty-six counties of Ireland (counties which were to become the Irish Free State) were Catholics. This figure has increased to over 95 per cent today. The proportion of committed and practising Catholics in Ireland marks it off from other EC countries with high Catholic populations. Before independence, government in Ireland was predominantly Protestant. The Catholic Church supported the nationalist movement and kept its distance from the government. After independence this aloofness was maintained. In other countries conflict arises between Church and State because the Church wishes to extend, maintain or defend its influence in the face of increased state activity. In the Free State, there was no major driving force for the secularisation of the new state. Some influential and senior clerics urged Irish governments for distinctly Catholic legislation. At the same time there was, however, no general desire on the Church's part to extend its authority because it was satisfied with the influence it already had.

In social welfare services, for instance, the Church has a stake which might seem extensive to visitors from Protestant countries. The state does not attempt to provide all such services itself. Many hospitals, orphanages, reformatories, and other welfare institutions are run by religious orders, with the aid of government grants and, to varying extents, under government control. The interpenetration of Church and state is seen most clearly in the field of education ... . In the first place education is not merely denominationally controlled: it is clerically controlled.[4]

In the conclusion of his definitive study Whyte looks at two opposing propositions on the influence of the Catholic Church in Ireland. On the one hand, he disagrees with the assertion that Ireland is a theocratic state 'in which the hierarchy has the final say on any matter in which it wishes to intervene'. He believes 'the total record does not show that Irish governments automatically defer to the hierarchy on any point on which the hierarchy chooses to speak'.[5] On the other hand, he feels that the notion that the Church is only one of a number of interest groups in society to be naive. For in the final analysis:

in a mainly Catholic country, the Catholic hierarchy has a weapon which no other group possesses: its authority over men's consciences. Most politicians on all sides of the house are committed Catholics, and accept the hierarchy's right to speak on matters of faith or morals. Even politicians who are personally indifferent on religious matters will recognise that the majority of the electorate are believers, and will act accordingly.[6]

In the past, the Church's predominance in Ireland had much to do with the social structure of the country. This consisted largely of small-scale rural communities. Priests found it relatively easy to exercise control over the inhabitants. This has changed as a result of urbanisation and industrialisation. The urban dwellers and the young are more willing to question established social and moral values. Further, increased disposable income, foreign travel, newspapers and television have led to an erosion of religiosity in Ireland.

The lessening of the Church's influence has been reflected in an increased demand for changes in the laws governing such issues as the availability of contraceptives and censorship. A survey published in September 1987 demonstrated again the widening gap between the attitudes to religion between the old and young and between those living in Dublin and those outside the capital. The influence of the Catholic Church over the morality of Irish people may have declined but the Church is still powerful and socially pervasive. Ninety-five per cent of all schools are under Catholic management, as are a significant number of social and health facilities. Parish clergy are active in all forms of community, sports and social organisations, especially in rural areas. The Church is involved in many aspects of Irish public life, which in other countries may be the exclusive province of secular authorities.

Conclusion

The structure and distribution of power in Ireland is similar to that in other liberal-democratic capitalist countries. Despite the fact that Ireland is, in formal terms, a meritocratic country, upward social mobility is restricted. As in other capitalist countries, the most powerful interest groups in Ireland are those concerned with the economy. Employers' organisations, in general, accept the state's management of the economy along capitalist lines. Employees' organisations, while mostly accepting the capitalist development of Ireland, are essentially concerned with defending the position of workers against low pay, poor working conditions, unfavourable terms of employment and unemployment. The economic, administrative and political elites share a common attachment to an essentially developmental image of the 'national' direction, but they are not as distant from the general population as elites in other countries.

There are many interest groups in Ireland not directly concerned with the economy. Several have existed for some time and campaign on general issues such as the preservation of the Irish language and culture. In recent years several campaigning groups have grown up to press their views on specific issues such as abortion and divorce. Other campaigns, such as that which developed in 1988 to oppose a fishing licence, bring previously non-political groups into public controversy for a short time. Similarly, environmental groups or those concerned to protect Ireland's architectural heritage are occasionally brought to the fore as a result of some issue which captures the general public's imagination. The non-economic organisation with the strongest influence in Ireland is the Catholic Church.

The interest groups press their views on public policy through a variety of methods. Usually the most effective groups are those whose views are heard away from the public gaze – those inside the policy 'community' which is dominated by ministers and civil servants. Street protests may demonstrate numerical strength or deep convictions but they often signal very little influence on the public policy.

References

1 G. Parry, *Political Elites*, London: Allen & Unwin, p. 13.

2 Whelan & Whelan, *Social Mobility in the Republic of Ireland*, p. 3.

3 P. Berresford-Ellis, *James Connolly: Selected Writings*, Harmondsworth: Penguin, 1981, p. 124.

4 J. Whyte, *Church and State in Modern Ireland, 1923–79*, pp. 16–17.

5 *Ibid.*, p. 369.

6 *Ibid.*, p. 368.

Further reading

R. Breen *et al.*, *Understanding Contemporary Ireland*, Dublin: Gill & Macmillan, 1990.

B. Chubb, *The Government and Politics of Ireland*, London: Longman, 1982.

P. Clancy *et al.* (eds.), *Ireland: a Sociological Profile*, Dublin: Institute of Public Administration, 1986.

C. Whelan & B. Whelan, *Social Mobility in the Republic of Ireland: A Comparative Perspective*, Dublin: Economic and Social Research Institute, 1984.

J. Whyte, *Church and State in Modern Ireland, 1923–79*, Dublin: Gill & Macmillan, 1971.

4
THE POLICY PROCESS

Some writers on government seek to distinguish between policy and administration or implementation. For this analysis, policy is defined as 'what governments do'; it is the cumulative impact of laws, rules, orders and incentives as they are formulated and carried out by civil servants, policemen, schoolteachers and others in authority. Sometimes the actual patterns of policy are very like the declarations made by politicians, parties and governments about how things should be done, but frequently they are not. This is not necessarily because politicians are devious or public servants disobedient. Rather, public policies are shaped by forces which are often outside politicians' own control. Those charged with enacting policy regularly overestimate their own control and influence on events. By the same token, the electorate and media ascribe too much power to the most obvious characters in the political drama, the Taoiseach, his ministers and their leading opponents in the Dáil.

In Ireland, for the reasons of electoral pressure and public expectations outlined in Chapter 2, many politicians present themselves to their constituents as able to alter significantly, in individual cases, what central or local government does. Thus many citizens believe that public policy in Ireland is the result of endless interventions by politicians in the operation of government departments, local authorities and other public bodies. The Department of Social Welfare, for example, deals with 40,000 representations and 4,000 parliamentary questions per year on its day-to-day operations. Explanations of public policy-making which concentrate on the brokerage activities of politicians are interesting, especially for what they tell us about elections. They are hardly adequate, however, to explain either the vast majority of decisions in which politicians play no direct part or, more importantly, the major decisions which transcend particular individual interests. In this chapter we will look at the process by which major national decisions like hospital closures, currency realignments or motorway construction are made and how the public service is organised to deal with such decision-making.

Ireland has undergone many important changes of policy direction, especially since the late 1950s. A long period of protectionism in economic policy, parity between the Irish currency and sterling and the near-total dependence on the British market for agricultural sales has ended. By 1985 more goods were exported to continental EC countries than to the UK. Over the same time foreign manufacturing investment has been encouraged, especially in highly technological industries such as computing. In the last fifteen years more than 850 overseas companies have set up in Ireland. Many policy changes have resulted from these new directions in economic strategy. While on the whole Irish prosperity has increased in recent decades as a result of such change, not all the effects have been positive socially, culturally or environmentally. So whose ideas fashioned these major national decisions, or, who sets the policy process in train?

One answer, which may be suggested from our discussion in Chapter 1, is 'nobody – in Ireland at least'. Certainly, as a small country with a heavy dependence on international trade and with many large multinational companies having Irish plants, decisions made in Chicago, New York, London, Tokyo and elsewhere can have immediate impact in Ireland. Even decisions to place new investment or orders in other countries with similar levels of development can have a direct impact on Irish public policy. Often such decisions are taken without reference to Ireland at all but for reasons of global commercial strategy. Nevertheless, patterns of employment, education and social expenditure in Ireland are directly affected. Thus, the decision to set up a factory in Spain may mean more emigration from the western county of

Mayo with resultant changes in school, medical and other provision. No Irish voice needs to be heard until decisions on which of Mayo's schools or hospital wards is to close is forced upon politicians or public servants by changed demography. Some outside influences, such as that of the Chernobyl nuclear accident, may have a long-term impact of an unpredictable nature on Ireland. To an extent, policy decisions represent reactions to outside pressures.

Of course, Ireland is not simply a recipient of outside influences, important though they are. Even in relation to multinational investment, public bodies such as the Industrial Development Authority examine, encourage, promote and decline offers of commercial developments. Some foreign plans, like the famous one to produce the De Lorean sports car in the Republic, are rejected as too risky. Others, such as a proposed facility in Kerry to recycle industrial waste, are turned down on environmental grounds. Nevertheless, most of the time Ireland's economy is open to foreign as well as domestic investment initiatives. Many decisions on Irish public policy are in effect conditioned by this reality. The emphasis in recent education policy upon computer literacy, for example, reflects the demands of international investment. Similarly, the policy of retrenchment in government spending, adopted by Irish cabinets in the late 1980s, was largely conditioned by currency and interest-rate changes over which there was little domestic control.

To recognise the importance of outside influence is not to ignore autonomous Irish action. Not everyone would see Ireland's current economic status or its social policies as primarily predetermined. Critics of the policies of recent government, for example, point out that Ireland did not have to borrow money to support her public spending when the oil crisis of the mid-1970s radically upset the economics of the world. The role of Irish actors must also be assessed. The shift of emphasis in Irish political and social policies of the late 1950s is popularly explained by the impact of a senior civil servant, T.K. Whitaker, and the then Taoiseach, Seán Lemass. These two men are credited with formulating, popularising and forming a coalition of support for a dramatic policy change in the form of new laws, new institutions and new thinking about economics, planning and development.

'Great men' do have an impact on the policy process, but their scope for innovation is limited by important political, economic and social considerations. Lemass, for example, had been a senior minister for years in administrations of a conservative and pro-tectionist kind. His espousal of radical measures on free trade, planning and relations with Northern Ireland must be seen in the light of the economic crisis and high emigration levels leading to pressure on his party's popularity. Fianna Fáil needed to react to the symptoms of a national malaise which threatened its legitimacy as 'the national party'. Further, Lemass's ideas drew directly on European and Christian social principles. His administrations were, in part, the Irish vehicle for a European-wide set of ideas fashionable among Christian Democrats. Whitaker was only one of a group of civil servants challenging the received wisdom of his civil service department. The policy process is thus an interaction between ideas, social and political pressures and opportunity in the context of the world economic order.

The popularity of the 'great man' explanation of the policy process arises from the simplification and dramatisation it allows in our understanding of events. In fact the process is far more mundane, complex and unsatisfactory. It involves many people and agencies marching to tunes of self-interest with remarkably little common purpose. In Ireland, most of the important partici-pants in the making of major national decisions belong to the higher levels of the government bureaucracy, economic pressure groups, major companies and senior politicians.

The number of people involved in policy-making at the highest level is less than 500. The assertion earlier that policy is what government does should, however, alert us to the significance of decisions made, and discretion exercised, by even the lowest public official. Formal and senior declarations of non-discrimi-nation against itinerants, for example, are not real descriptions of policy if patrolling *gardaí* regularly harass such people or if housing officers routinely ignore their plight. The government bureaucracy also includes many public servants who prefer to be seen as professionals rather than as bureaucrats.

'Professionals' frequently claim that their judgements are based on abstract and neutral ideas and are to that extent non-political. Thus, health policy is in part the pattern of priorities advocated by health board doctors and not just edicts from the Department of Health. When questioned about their decisions, doctors regularly talk of 'clinical judgement'. The scarce resources which they command, such as medicines and operating theatres, should be outside the public arena, because a doctor's priorities can only be judged by his peers. Though their use of resources for one treatment may deny them for another, doctors, like lawyers, engineers and other professionals in the public service, would not regard themselves as part of a political process. Further, even though governments set the overall spending limits, the precise allocation of funds to different hospitals and specialisms has been devolved to local health board members. Health policy is, therefore, significantly influenced by boards of councillors, medical and paramedical professionals and ministerial appointees.

In this chapter we will be concentrating on major national decisions. In Ireland, these are largely the result of initiatives within government departments. Where legislation is required to enforce new policies, this is secured by the government's majority in the legislature. Both major parties run on tightly authoritarian lines so that Irish governments can retain control, even with very small majorities, or even in a minority if the opposition is divided.

Government departments are organised on functional lines to cover the major areas of policy such as agriculture, health and foreign affairs (see Table 4.1). The administrative cost of running departments, as opposed to providing services, is about £700m. or over 10 per cent of the 1991 estimate of all government spending. The Department of Finance occupies a key position as the custodian of government money. Each department is staffed by civil servants, the most senior of whom is called the secretary. Departmental secretaries, their assistant secretaries and principals, are the most powerful public servants in the government bureaucracy. Their ideas of what is desirable, possible and, to a degree, politically advantageous for the government to do, is most

Table 4.1 *Government departments*

Department of Agriculture & Food
Department of Defence
Department of Education
Department of Environment
Department of Finance
Department of Foreign Affairs
Department of the Gaeltacht
Department of Health
Department of Tourism & Transport
Department of Energy
Department of Communications
Department of the Marine
Department of Industry & Commerce
Department of Justice
Department of Labour
Department of Social Welfare
Department of the Taoiseach

---

influential in determining what is done. The secretaries are the main channel for civil service advice available to ministers and though ministers frequently change, their advisers do not. Because of their influence and Ireland's relatively unimpressive economic progress, many commentators have been critical of their social vision and openness to new ideas. Such comments have often centred on their supposedly narrow educational background, and their cautious outlook, encouraged by slow promotion and lack of private sector experience.

All the present secretaries are men and, under recent changes, may normally only hold office for a maximum of seven years. As we saw in Chapter 3, their career paths, typically, will have been entirely in the civil service, though in future the top posts may be opened to wider competition. Since leaving school they may well have gained a degree through part-time study. Those on the senior ranks below secretary may have entered the service after university but still at a junior grade. Civil servants themselves see that the hierarchical system has some dampening effect on initiative but feel that caution, even parsimony, is a virtue in a servant of the public. Though some management techniques may have been learned from the private sector, the civil servants' view of the world is probably different. Public service, in the view of senior civil servants, remains a bastion of integrity, national responsibility and hard work which bears laudable comparison to other sectors of Irish public life. It is indeed difficult to argue with such a view but it may well be that such a self-image makes the senior civil servant somewhat unresponsive to new ideas from business, academia, pressure groups or elsewhere.

The exact list of tasks carried out by, and the title of, each government department varies as political fashion, administrative convenience or government responsibilities change. There remains, however, a fairly identifiable core of departments which have been involved with agriculture, defence, education, local government, foreign affairs and other major areas since the early years of the state. It would be odd if, as individuals and collectively, public officials who had worked in these areas did not develop coherent and generalised views of where the public interest lies. Even modest, self-effacing civil servants would presumably resist, to some extent, challenges to the 'departmental line' from their nominal superiors – government ministers. Of course, ministers ultimately have to prevail if open clashes of opinion occur, and they too have ideas of public priorities. Further departmental posts at the top three levels are no longer automatically filled from within its ranks following the introduction of more competition in 1984.

When a single party forms a government its ideas may be fairly broad and open to change through cabinet reconsideration and civil service advice. In the case of a coalition, however, some distinct policy ideas may have been determined by prior negotiation between the parties and subsequent civil service reservations may count for little. Individual ministers may see it as their primary task to 'deliver' on a policy promise even in the face of reservations from within their own party in order to ensure that a coalition arrangement survives. Thus, for example, the Minister of Finance whose party, Fine Gael, was in coalition with Labour, introduced a wealth tax in 1975 despite pressure from some of his back bench and even from Fine Gael cabinet colleagues, in part to ensure the government's survival. Subsequently, estate duties were abolished by the same government to placate Fine Gael supporters. The civil service is understood to have opposed both these tax reforms. In the case of the wealth tax, however, they had to accept the cabinet's basic principles and the minister's modifications to assuage party opinion. The Department of Finance's influence was confined to advising the ministers on technicalities. As we will discuss below, however, ministers can only attend directly to a small proportion of government business.

Most of the time the policy process in Ireland is dominated by civil servants acting within the broad parameters set by the government of the day. The better a party's preparation for government while in opposition or the more specific its public proposals, the less role the civil servants can be expected to play in policy formulation. Formally, and importantly in legal terms, the orders, advice and publicly expressed opinions of civil servants are all in the name of the minister. Under the Ministers and Secretaries Act 1924 the minister is the 'corporation sole' of the department. All legal powers are conferred on him and used in his name. Thus phrases such as 'I am instructed by the minister to' or 'the minister requests' appear on documents that the minister may never have seen or of which he is only vaguely aware. Since the same formal language also appears when the minister is showing a direct personal interest in an area of policy, to the outsider the authority of the document is the same. Senior civil servants communicate, not only for their minister by letter but also informally through networks of contacts in every aspect of public life. A retired Secretary to the Department of Finance wrote:

Only those who have worked close to Ministers have any idea of the many demands on their time. One indication of the limited amount of time which a Minister can devote to the affairs of his Department is the difficulty which the *official* head of the Department (the secretary) and his senior colleagues experience in obtaining a meeting with him. Perhaps this difficulty is accentuated in the Department of Finance, whose Minister is subject to unusually varied pressures; it is certainly *not* a problem of personalities since the difficulty does not vary much with different Ministers.[1]

As they do not personally build houses, teach children or manufacture goods, civil servants must keep a check on public policy by monitoring those who do. Information is crucial and the skill of interpreting it central to civil servants. For this reason their work is dominated by a stream of official figures, reports from their juniors, personal impressions, politicians' and citizens' letters, gossip and media speculation. Their centrality in these networks of information is a strength and a source of vulnerability for civil servants. How do they make sense of it all? The model of the world they employ is a vitally important element in how policy is formed and reformed. This is why the departmental line, the civil servants' backgrounds and the openness to fresh ideas are important.

There is a constitutional limit of fifteen on the number of cabinet ministers and they may be assisted by up to fifteen ministers of state. All must be members of the Oireachtas (two may be from the Seanad). To form an idea of how difficult it is for ministers to keep track of the areas of policy for which they are responsible, it is useful to look at the structure of even a small department. The primary functions of the Department of Foreign Affairs are advising the government on Ireland's external relations, being a channel for official communications with foreign governments and international agencies and monitoring developments in Northern Ireland. European Community business is a significant burden for the Department. About 130 people above the level of third secretary are based in headquarters in Dublin. Several hundred more employees, many of them not Irish, are dispersed in various forms of official representation around the world. There are over forty separate embassies, consulates and their equivalents.

It would be unreasonable to expect ministers to be *au fait* with all their Departments' work. Nevertheless, any task is liable to become the focus of public controversy. Thus, for example, the routine task of issuing passports, to which few Ministers for Foreign Affairs have given much attention, became a political embarrassment when in 1987 it was revealed that gross irregularities in this function had occurred at the London embassy. The Minister for Foreign Affairs was called on to give an account of how such a situation 'was allowed to happen'.

More important for policy-making is the rivalry that exists between departments. Thus, to take a Foreign Affairs example again, European Community matters have been the responsibility of that Department since the negotiations for Ireland's entry. Nevertheless, the Department's views, tutored by the exigencies of diplomacy, can only be brought to fruition if they prevail over the possibly dissimilar interests of those responsible for finance and agriculture. To an extent departments 'capture' areas of discretion or advice. If responsibility is given to another department, control over the flow of information, prestige and power are lost. There may, for example, be conflict between the Department of Foreign Affairs and the Department of Industry and Commerce in regard to negotiations on trade treaties with foreign governments or international organisations.

In many government departments it is difficult to assess the impact of policy other than in terms of increased service provision. Whether Ireland is better educated, defended, housed or provided for in terms of health and welfare is hard to gauge. A reasonable measure may be, however, what is spent on these services. Thus civil servants, who come to identify an increase in their service with the general national good, may be motivated to maximise their departmental budgets. Such motives, together with the understandable personal interest in more salary, promotion and prestige have, according to their critics, become significant reasons for the seemingly inexorable growth of public expenditure.

Although politicians in government are only directly involved in a small proportion of the policy for which they are 'responsible', that proportion is often the most controversial. The public odium which attends failure or insensitivity in policy implementation descends on the politicians in office. Cabinet ministers are especially vulnerable to criticism. By contrast, they must also be seen to receive the plaudits for policy successes and popular initiatives. There are few more prized opportunities for a politician than the opening of a factory, new road or hospital in or near his or her constituency. A department which fails to alert its minister to a possibly embarrassing development or potential opportunity to be associated with a success would be open to sharp criticism. On the other hand, departments rely on their ministers to secure their position in the inter-departmental rivalry on policies and responsibilities. For a civil service department a good minister is one who wins winnable battles in cabinet or elsewhere, who makes decisions on the files sent to him or her and who stands up for the officials in times of criticism. For a minister, a good department is one where the opportunities for good publicity are substantial. For a short time, if the public mood is sympathetic, a minister may even gain in popularity by being seen to take 'unpopular' decisions. The public tolerance of cut-backs is short, however.

The supposed dichotomy between policy and administration is one to which civil servants often point. They claim that once broad and clearly political choices are made by ministers they merely facilitate their implementation. To this extent civil servants are politically neutral administrators while politicians are the effective policy-makers. This model of the policy process is rather like the legal description. Many analysts of the policy process recognise it to be of limited use, but it remains a powerful ideal. Attempts have been made, therefore, to create a distinct policy-making section within each government department, called the *aireacht*, to secure the clearer identification and separation of functions. Those not in this small and senior group could then develop systems of administration free of 'political' considerations.

The *aireacht* idea was first put forward in 1969 and was to a large extent cold-shouldered by both civil servants and politicians at the time. Nevertheless, the *aireacht* model has been influential, particularly on official and other would-be reformers of the current system. Most departments now have specialist units for planning, finance, organisation and personnel. Basic to the reformers' views is the idea that better policy would be made by politicians and senior officials who were freed from day-to-day responsibility for administration *per se*. This approach received important support with the publication in September 1985 of the White Paper, *Serving the Country Better:*

There are, in fact, two broad functions which the civil service performs: the delivery of a wide range of services to the public; and the formulation of policy, and advice and planning on behalf of the Government ... . In most departments there is no clear or satisfactory separation between the policy advisory functions and the day-to-day management of executive activities. As long as this remains so, there will not be sufficient emphasis either on the managerial concern with getting results, reducing costs and improving the service to the public or on the development of corporate planning and long term policy analysis.[2]

Despite this endorsement, the 1985 White Paper has not been followed by any significant change in the pattern of civil service organisation of day-to-day work.

In all years, but particularly during the recent crisis in Ireland's public finances, other areas of policy-making are overshadowed by the formulation of the government's budgetary proposals. The timetable for completing the budget may be affected by elections or other political crises. Typically, however, each summer, government departments prepare their plans for the year beginning the following January. These plans will concern spending increases or cuts both on the current and capital accounts. Each department's plans reflect its priorities either as enunciated by its ministers or put forward by civil servants themselves. In many cases new ideas may have been formulated in the department for some time in the hope that a 'sympathetic' minister will adopt them.

Usually one year's departmental budget will be similar to the previous year's, with changes confined to small adjustments to established services and only a few new departures. Most attention is given to these new items by the Department of Finance and ministers first in a cabinet sub-committee and then in full cabinet. Although the budgetary process is an annual one many aspects are legally, politically or otherwise committed for a longer period, so change is confined to a small proportion of actual expenditure. This pattern of incremental change has, however, been radically altered since the formation of the Fianna Fáil government in 1987.

Departments with large budgets, such as Education and Health, were obliged to make sweeping economies involving the abandonment of previously safe projects with the loss of health service and teaching jobs. For example, in 1988 the Minister of Health set a target of 2,000 health service redundancies. Though the public finances were improving, a similar programme of cuts was set out for 1989, though this time social welfare and local government suffered most. Since 1987 the annual budgetary process starts with a review of policy involving ministers, senior civil servants and a private sector economist which sets targets (usually cuts) within which departments must operate. The impact of these changes has been to reduce government expenditure from 53 per cent of GNP in 1986 to 42 per cent in 1990.

Such tight budgeting involved severe competition for the remaining funds and intense competition between sections within each department. The major rows, however, are usually between spending departments and the Department of Finance, which take place during the autumn months, when detailed submissions are considered. The Department of Finance aggregates the figures and compares them with the government's capacity to raise taxes or borrow money at home or abroad. Inevitably the Department seeks to reduce expenditure by questioning the need for, details of, or costing associated with each department's proposals. After the haggling is over, Finance publishes details of the proposed expenditure in January. The Minister for Finance then prepares his own budgetary proposals which outline how the government intends to raise the money to meet its bills.

In assessing the level of taxation the Department of Finance works closely with the Revenue Commissioners who are responsible for its collection. The Dáil discusses the government's plans but few changes are made before the necessary legislation is passed. Once the cabinet and civil servants, working in confidence, have arrived at a pattern of expenditure and taxation involving intense bargaining and compromise, it is difficult to find room for significant adjustments. Further, for any government to be unsuccessful in carrying its budget in a Dáil vote would be a very serious political embarrassment and, by convention, would lead to a general election. Major changes in the budget have been forced on governments in the past, especially when the disposition of parties is close. Deputies have forced significant adjustments to both Fianna Fáil and coalition governments' budget proposals, notably in respect of taxation of farmers. In 1987 the minority Fine Gael government was defeated on its budget and subsequently lost office. Nevertheless, major changes to a government's proposals are very infrequent.

The budgetary cycle is completed when each department's accounts are audited by the Comptroller and Auditor-General and his staff. The Dáil's Public Accounts Committee goes over the Comptroller and Auditor-General's report in some detail with the accounting officer (usually the secretary) of each department. The Committee is usually chaired by an opposition deputy so any irregularities in the accounts are carefully checked.

The budgetary process puts an emphasis on several crucial and annual deadlines or meetings at which decisions are finalised. Thus policy-makers can themselves become over concerned with their ability to defend proposals in the short term. Most of the government's expenditure is, however, committed on a continuing basis so a lot of attention is paid to those budget items that can be adjusted quickly. This means that some kinds of expenditure are especially vulnerable to change for *ad hoc* short-term reasons and this may lead to serious misallocation of scarce public resources.

The civil service has attempted to adopt methods of working that take in the medium and long-term financial planning outlook. Since 1 March 1991 all departments have introduced a system of delegated administrative budgets which allows greater spending flexibility and adjustments from one year's budget to the next. It is possible that this initiative may be more successful than its predecessors. For example between 1977 and 1981 a new department was formed to concentrate on economic planning and development, but as resources became scarcer the Department of Finance reasserted its influence and financial outlook. Similarly, at times of cutbacks in expenditure, 'spending' ministers with political skill will make a particularly significant impact both in defending some proposed targets and opposing others.

The Department of Finance's predominant position in the annual budgetary process is only part of the reason for its influence. The Department, which is the only one mentioned in the Constitution, is involved in all aspects of economic policy and planning. It negotiates Ireland's trade agreements and deals with the European Monetary System, tax harmonisation and the like. It does, however, have rivals. The Department of the Taoiseach is an increasingly important part of the policy-making process.

The Taoiseach has always been a most influential policy-maker. He is, after all, the leader of the main government party. He also chooses his colleagues, though this power is effectively modified under a coalition, and it is to him that the public look to champion the government's cause and offer leadership. Until 1982 this Department remained small and non-interventionist. Under recent holders of the post of Taoiseach the Department has grown in size and so, too, has the scope of its direct responsibility.

The Taoiseach, like other ministers, may appoint special advisers with a party-political background. Their tenure is dependent on the life of the government. In 1987 Charles Haughey introduced four such advisors, including Fianna Fáil's former Head of Research. Similarly the former Fianna Fáil Press Officer was appointed government press secretary. The Taoiseach's civil service private office staff does not automatically change as a new incumbent arrives. The Department of the Taoiseach includes about four ministers of state including the Government Chief Whip. Thus the Taoiseach's team have a crucial hold on the legislative programme and party discipline.

Particularly under single party governments, the Taoiseach has been able to exercise forceful leadership and close management of the government's overall business. The Department of the Taoiseach is potentially the most powerful Department of all. The leadership style of one recent Taoiseach led to the phrase 'Uno duce, una voce' entering everyday Irish political parlance. Advice to the Taoiseach is still provided by functional departments, but it is now more closely scrutinised.

The role of the Taoiseach as Ireland's representative at the European Council has added to the centrality of his Department.

The Department of Foreign Affairs has also gained prominence as a result of Ireland's EC membership. Ireland's permanent representation in Brussels is dominated by Foreign Affairs although other departments, particularly Agriculture, are represented. Because many policies have their origins in the European Commission, a close watching brief is kept and representations made by Irish civil servants based in Brussels.

The budgetary process, with its tendency to encourage piecemeal and incremental change, departmental rivalry, civil service conservativism and caution, acts as a barrier to the establishment of radically new public policies. Despite the rhetoric of party policies in Ireland and elsewhere, public policies are more notable for continuity than change. New ideas take time to find sufficient acceptance among politicians, bureaucrats and the public and even longer to effect state provision. Small countries, such as Ireland, often wait to learn from experiments and innovation elsewhere. Obviously in Ireland's case the example of the UK is a powerful influence.

Some policies have not changed in terms of broad principles even since independence. Most notably the social welfare system, which accounts for 27 per cent of current government spending and is run by the government department with the largest budget, has developed in a piecemeal manner, with no major review since 1908. Policy developments have depended very much on the hectic bargaining of the budgetary process with change often finalised only in the hours before the Budget speech. In 1986, however, the Report of the Commission on Social Welfare set out new principles to guide the development of a new system of social welfare. Major reports of this kind, on areas such as taxation or public sector management itself, do provide a vehicle for new ideas. Their influence is, however, ultimately constrained by party and bureaucratic politics, as well as the lack of broad public consensus. The same is true of less elaborate forms of consultation and advice which are submitted to the government by private and semi-official bodies such as the National Economic and Social Council (NESC).

The NESC was established in 1973 specifically to provide

advice to government, through the Taoiseach, from employers, trade unionists and others. The NECS's chairman is the Secretary of the Department of the Taoiseach so it has better access than most pressure groups but the government does receive policy representation from a broad range of sources. Some reports, books and memoranda are influential and do mark turning-points in particular areas of policy; others help change the general climate of opinion about particular policies. Critics maintain, however, that Irish policy-makers, whether politicians or civil servants, are not sufficiently open to new ideas. Only when those ideas come from powerful pressure groups such as the major producer organisations are they regularly influential.

One of the main planks in the nationalist movement in Ireland was the desire to control market conditions and build up Irish industry. This was Fianna Fáil's main economic strategy. Thus, when that party took office in 1932 it put tariffs on imports in order to encourage Irish entrepreneurs to set up manufacturing businesses. This policy certainly helped to widen the Irish manufacturing base by protecting it from outside competition. Reliance on the domestic market, however, kept industrial concerns relatively small-scale and uncompetitive in international markets. There were also essential economic functions which did not attract private investment. In these cases the government established semi-autonomous state-sponsored bodies. Examples of these include the Electricity Supply Board, CIE (the public transport authority), Bord na Móna (the peat development authority), Aer Lingus (the national airline) and Bord Gáis Eireann (the Irish gas board). The commercial state-sponsored bodies operate basically like private companies in that they are expected to make profits to cover their operations and expansion. Today, the ninety state-sponsored bodies employ almost 96,000 people, about a third of the public service.

The heads of these larger semi-state or state-sponsored bodies have a clear and direct role in public policy. They have open communications with ministers and senior civil servants in their 'parent' departments. As commercial enterprises, they invest large sums of money in important infrastructural projects and the government takes a close interest in their plans. The government appoints directors or council members to state-sponsored companies' boards or councils.

The political importance of some companies arises from their dependence on public funding and others, especially those involved in the promotion of economic development, from their influence on job creation. The Industrial Development Authority, Bord Fáilte (the Tourist Board) and the Shannon Free Airport Development Company are all state-sponsored bodies involved in economic development. To an extent they compete with each other to develop plans, secure investment and influence government policy in the Department of Industry and Commerce. On taking office in 1987 the Fianna Fáil government viewed such competition as wasteful and unnecessary. All three agencies have had their responsibilities rationalised and their influence may well decrease. Some non-commercial state-sponsored bodies, such as An Foras Forbartha (the National Institute for Physical Planning and Construction Research) and the Health Education Bureau, were abolished. Civil service departments have taken over tasks previously the responsibility of such agencies.

Conclusions

In this chapter, we have seen that public policy is constrained by private interests and commercial realities which are shaped by Ireland's place in the world economic order. Demographic, climatic and environmental factors also have a role in determining what governments do. Within these constraints, Ireland does have important decisions to make. To the extent that the political system has autonomy, powerful figures in public life can make a significant impact given the political and economic opportunity. Too much emphasis is placed, however, on the explanatory value of 'great persons" actions.

The making of Irish public policy is dominated by a relatively small number of politicians and high-level civil servants. The process is often an incremental and annual one though there have been a number of radical turning-points. Economic policy, taxation and government expenditure are central to the concerns of all recent Irish governments and on these issues there is a broad range of consensus among the politicians and in the civil service. On most policies, therefore, the bureaucrats are very influential. Politicians ultimately take public responsibility and their attention to policy is greatest when either controversy and/or specific political commitments are high.

References

1 *Administration, Vol.* 30, No. 4, 1980, pp. 53–4.
2 *Serving the Country Better,* Dublin: Stationery Office, 1985, pp. 5–6.

Further reading

T. J. Barrington, *The Irish Administrative System,* Dublin: Institute of Public Administration, 1980.

B. Chubb, *Government and Politics of Ireland,* Harlow: Longman, 1982.

S. Dooney & J. O'Toole, *Irish Government Today,* Dublin: Gill & Macmillan, 1991.

J. Lee, *Ireland 1912–1985: Politics and Society,* Cambridge: Cambridge University Press, 1989.

5

THE CONSTITUTION AND THE LAW

The present Constitution, Bunreacht na hEireann, came into operation on 29 December 1937. Its fiftieth anniversary was the occasion of the renewal of the debate about what such a document should contain and how frequently it should be changed. The Labour Party, the Workers' Party and the Progressive Democrats have called for a new document while the other parties favour a process of revision. It is likely, therefore, that the debate will continue for some time. This chapter looks at the provisions of the Constitution, its origins and the wider system of law of which it is a part.

The Constitution

The principles of liberal democracy were fashioned and tested by the French and American revolutions at the end of the eighteenth century. The rule of law and the pivotal position of the constitution are of utmost importance in this system of government.

Liberal democratic theory grew up in reaction to the rule of the many by the few. At its base was the notion of individual liberty. For the theorists the power of government comes from the people. They wished to see government representing the will of its people, through consultation, election and plebiscite. But it was also realised that if a tyranny of a minority could exist then so too could a tyranny of a majority. The freedom of the individual had to be guaranteed. An agreed set of rules and standards, which could be used as an objective test for the protection of individuals against government, was established under the rule of law. The essential basis of this law was the written constitution.

A constitution does several things:

1. It outlines the structure of government. The liberal–democratic form of government is distinguished by the separation of power into the legislature, the executive, and the judiciary.
2. It reflects and codifies the values and beliefs of society.
3. It is often a statement of intent of what the people would like their society to be. This is particularly so in countries which are in the process of great social or political upheaval.

Because the constitution is the supreme source of law, it is usually made more difficult to change than other laws. Often the wording can only be altered when the people have been consulted by referendum. A constitution is usually also open to judicial review. Although the words cannot be changed by judges, the meaning of words, or the meaning of phrases, can be. In effect, new rights and obligations can be created. This can sometimes be contrary to what was previously assumed to be permissible under the constitution. This aspect of constitutional change will be looked at more closely below.

Newly-independent countries frequently experience an initial period of relatively rapid constitutional change. This was the case with Ireland, which has had three constitutions, one in 1919, another in 1922 and then the present one, adopted in 1937. The twenty-six counties were given the official status of a republic by the Republic of Ireland Act 1948.

The first and second Constitutions

It is noteworthy that while the leaders of the Irish independence struggle were attempting to throw off British rule, their 1919 Constitution accepted the Westminster parliamentary system as a model for the new Irish government. Although the members of Sinn Féin asserted in principle and in practice their right to armed struggle, they were schooled in, and accepted, the ideals of constitutional politics. The Constitution of 1919 reflected the predominantly liberal–democratic nature of the independence movement and the influence of Sinn Féin's legal advisors, who were mostly trained in the British legal system.

The second Constitution, which was called the 'The Constitution of the Irish Free State', also followed the British model. It set up a bicameral legislature consisting of a lower house (Dáil) and an upper house (Seanad), with a cabinet government responsible to the Dáil.

The Seanad was comprised of members elected by a restricted franchise and others appointed by the head of the government. There were some differences with Britain. Full adult suffrage was introduced, six years in advance of Britain, and election by proportional representation was prescribed. Other important differences included measures to make the government more responsible to the people. There were provisions for the initiation of legislation from outside the Oireachtas and for the instigation of a referendum to test public opinion on legislation. Following the example of the written constitutions of France and America, the Free State Constitution also included a declaration of rights. These included freedom of expression, religion and association, habeas corpus and the inviolability of the citizen's home.

When in 1932 Fianna Fáil was elected to government, it was clear that the Constitution would come under critical review because the Constitution of the Irish Free State was based on the Anglo-Irish Treaty. De Valera intended to remove all the vestiges of British control in Ireland from the Free State Constitution. The years between 1933 and the introduction of a totally new constitution in 1937 were used to get rid of what Fianna Fáil considered the most objectionable parts of the 1922 Constitution. The links with Britain were reduced, with the removal of the oath to the Crown and the virtual abolition of the office of Governor-General. In 1936 de Valera was able to take advantage of the abdication of Edward VIII to remove the Crown from the Irish Free State Constitution. In 1937 he introduced Bunreacht na hEireann, the third Irish Constitution.

The 1937 Constitution

This Constitution mirrored de Valera's views and represented a further break with Britain. 'In that Constitution' he later said, 'the traditional aspirations of our people, of national independence, national unity and the unfettered control of their domestic and foreign affairs have been set as the basic principles of the law by which we are to be governed' (radio broadcast, 29 December 1937).

The system of government was in the mould of other liberal democratic states:

(a) Sovereignty lay with the people.
(b) The Head of State, the President, was to be elected.
(c) Parliament was to consist of two houses.
(d) There would be a separate and independent judiciary.

Like other written constitutions, Bunreacht na hEireann contained positive social principles and guaranteed certain individual rights. A definite Catholic ethos pervades these provisions. In the articles on the family and its protection, particularly the ban on divorce, and in its attitude to women and their role in society, the Constitution reflects Catholic teaching of the 1930s.

The President

As Head of State, the President performs a range of formal acts of government as well as being the symbol of the state in ceremonial functions both at home and abroad. The Irish President is not the Head of Government as in the USA or France. The Head of Government in Ireland is the Taoiseach. Nor is the Irish President the source of governmental power, as is the British monarchy. De Valera claimed the President 'is there to guard the people's rights and mainly to guard the Constitution'. The President's role as representative of the people is signified by the provision that he be directly elected every seven years. The President may be re-elected once only. On four occasions the main political parties have agreed on one candidate and no election was necessary. Thus, for example, President Hillary re-nominated himself at the expiry of his first term of seven years in 1983 and was unopposed. The last election was in November 1990 when Mary Robinson became the seventh President of Ireland.

The President has essentially six powers to enable her to carry out her guardian role, of which the first four below are the most important.

1. He or she may refer any bill to the Supreme Court to test if it contains anything repugnant to the Constitution. If a government wishes to proceed with a bill declared repugnant to the Constitution it has to submit it to a referendum, thus giving the people the final say.

2. If a majority of the members of Seanad Eireann and not less than one-third of the members of the Dáil petition the President not to sign a bill, on the grounds that it contains a proposal of such national importance that the will of the people should be sought, he or she may decide to do so. The bill will then only be signed if it is approved in a referendum or by a new Dáil elected after a dissolution and general election.

3. The President may convene a meeting of the Houses of the Oireachtas; this is intended to cover the emergency situation where those whose job it is to call a meeting cannot or will not.

4. The Dáil is summoned and dissolved by the President on the advice of the Taoiseach. If, however, the Taoiseach has ceased to retain the support of the majority of TDs, the President may refuse a dissolution, giving the Dail a chance to elect a different Taoiseach and avoiding a general election. In practice, when a Taioscach is defeated on a matter of confidence and asks for a dissolution, it is granted.

5. If the Dail and government wish to restrict the time a bill may be considered by the Seanad, the President must concur.

6. The President has a minor role in the disputes between the Ceann Comhairle (Chairman of the Dáil) and the Seanad about whether a specific bill is a 'money bill', i.e. one on which the Seanad's role is very restricted.

There is little scope for the President to exercise anything but negative power. The office has remained largely ceremonial and above controversy. On the one occasion that the Presidency did invoke controversy, in 1976, the President resigned in order to keep conflict out of the office.

President O Dalaigh, acting entirely properly in terms of the responsibilities of his office, referred the Emergency Powers Bill of the coalition government to the Supreme Court for a decision on its constitutionality. Although the Bill could not be declared unconstitutional because the government had proclaimed a state of emergency, the President believed that the Court had the power to enquire into the existence of a genuine state of emergency. Although some government members were privately critical of this action, there was little public concern about the matter. The Minister for Defence, Patrick Donegan, however, claimed that the President was a 'thundering disgrace' because of his actions. President O Dalaigh thought this 'outrageous criticism' had brought his office into disrepute. The refusal of the Taoiseach to accept Donegan's resignation made it seem that he was standing by his minister's remarks. So the President resigned. Clearly President O Dalaigh had been put in an impossible position by the government. The offence was compounded by the fact that the minister's remarks were made at an army function – the supreme command of the defence forces is vested in the President. The exercise of the supreme command is regulated by the Defence Act 1954; nevertheless, officers of the defence forces hold their commissions from the President.

The Seanad

The upper house, Seanad Eireann, has sixty members. It has a subordinate position in the Oireachtas. De Valera, effective author of Bunreacht na hEireann, felt the real value of the Seanad lay in checking, redrafting and amending legislation.

The Seanad's membership was originally intended to reflect the principal of vocationalism. The idea that government should be made up of representatives from interested groups in society held great sway in Catholic and conservative movements in the

1930s. In reality, the Seanad is dominated by party politics: eleven senators are nominated by the Taoiseach and the other forty-nine elected. Three senators each are elected by the graduates of the University of Dublin and the National University of Ireland (though, within the enabling provisions of the Seventh Amendment of the Constitution, the arrangements for these six senators may be revised). The other forty-three are elected from five panels of candidates containing people with knowledge and service in the following areas: Culture and Education (5); Agriculture (11); Labour (11); Industry and Commerce (9); and Public Administration (7). The electorate for Seanad elections was amended, in the Seanad Electoral (Panel Members) Act 1947, to include all members of the Oireachtas and county and county borough councillors.

Powers of the Seanad

The Seanad's powers are limited to revising and clarifying bills, plus some constitutional duties and rights. It has no power of substance, especially in relation to financial matters. The Seanad is often used as a stopping-point for retiring TDs or those who failed to get re-elected. It has also been useful for would-be TDs to make an initial entry on to the parliamentary scene.

The Dáil and the government

According to the Constitution, the government will consist of not less than seven and not more than fifteen members. The Taoiseach, the Tanaiste (deputy prime minister) and the Minister for Finance must be members of the Dáil. All other members of the government must be members of the Oireachtas, although a maximum of two can be from the Seanad. Ministers have the right to attend and to speak in either house. The government is responsible to the Dáil alone.

The lower house of the Oireachtas, Dáil Eireann, has varied in size from 128 seats to 166 at present. (There has to be a TD for every 20,000 to 30,000 electors.) The country is at present divided into forty-one constituencies and their number must be revised at least once every twelve years to take account of population changes. Such a review was completed in October 1988 . The Dáil lasts for a maximum of five years. A general election must take place not later than thirty days after the dissolution and the newly-elected Dáil must meet within thirty days from the polling date.

The ministers of government

Usually each member of government becomes the head of one of the departments of state and sometimes two. Apart from the members of government there are also up to a maximum of fifteen ministers of state who assist their government ministers in parliamentary and departmental duties. They must be members of the Oireachtas and have in practice been members of the Dáil. A minister of state in the Department of the Taoiseach, with special responsibilities as Government Chief Whip, attends government meetings as of right. The other ministers of state are occasionally invited to attend if an item within their particular area of responsibility warrants it.

The government has exclusive initiative in matters of finance. Article 17 of the Constitution states: 'Dáil Eireann may not pass any vote or resolution and no law shall be enacted for the appropriation of revenue or other public moneys, unless the purpose of the appropriation shall have been recommended to Dáil Eireann by a message from the Government signed by the Taoiseach.' As noted above, the power the Seanad has over finances is limited: it may make recommendations but not substantive changes.

Amendments to the Constitution

From 1941 until 1972 Bunreacht na hEireann remained unchanged. Once a transitional period for easier amendment was ended, Ireland's Constitution was essentially settled. It can only be changed by referendum, of which there have been several in recent years. In total since 1937 there have been ten amendments,

Table 5.1 *Constitutional referenda from 1937*

Date	Subject
1937	Plebiscite to adopt Constitution
1954*	Changing PR voting system
1968*	Size of Dáil constituencies
1968*	Changing PR voting system
1972	Membership of European Community
1972	Lowering voting age
1972	Changing reference to position of Catholic Church
1979	Adoption
1979	Seanad university seats
1983	Protection of unborn
1984	Extension of voting for non-citizens
1986*	Provision for divorce
1987	Single European Act

Note: * = Defeated

including two passed before June 1941 which did not require popular approval (see Table 5. 1).

Judicial review

One of the major developments concerning Bunreacht na hEireann is the way it has been changed through interpretation rather than any changes in its wording. The basic provision for judicial review has always been present in the Constitution. Article 15.4.1 forbids the Oireachtas from passing any law repugnant to the Constitution. Article 34.3.2 gives this power of review to the High Court, while Article 34.3.3 allows its decisions on such questions to be appealed to the Supreme Court. This power was not used, however, in any positive sense until the mid-1960s.

Causes of change

From the 1960s onwards there was a realisation by dynamic Irish jurists and others that the Constitution was a legal document, guaranteeing fundamental rights to individuals. There are a number of reasons why lawyers did not see such possibilities before this time:

1. The lawyers up to the mid-1960s were all schooled in the British tradition. Britain does not have a written constitution and depends instead on a form of 'common law'. Thus, it lacks any fundamental rights provisions or any written positive social justice criteria. The sovereignty of parliament in making laws is considered absolute.

2. The earlier years of Bunreacht na hEireann were dominated by the Second World War and internal subversion such as the IRA border campaign in the 1950s. This was a period of increased security legislation, a state of emergency and, during the war, a standing military court. An atmosphere existed which militated against the development of citizens' rights. The situation changed in the 1960s. The security situation improved and emergency legislation was no longer required (although it remained on the statute book).

3. More positively, Ireland's economic growth and prosperity increased significantly in the 1960s. The higher living standards helped stem the flow of emigration. Consequently, the population became both younger and increasingly influenced by more cosmopolitan ideas.

4. Further, there was specific change within the legal profession itself. Standards of legal education improved. Many students went to law schools in America and recognised the constitutional parallels between the USA and Ireland. New people began to dominate in the court structure and by about 1970 there was a majority of 'progressive' or 'liberal' judges in the Supreme Court. Judges were increasingly willing to reinterpret the Constitution and, at the same time, more groups sought to pursue their interests by recourse to the courts.

Results of change

The main result of judicial interpretation has been the augmenting of individual rights. Articles 40 to 44 of the Constitution list fundamental rights which 'the State guarantees in its laws to respect, and, as far as practicable, ... to defend and vindicate' (Article 40.3.1). These include equality before the law; personal liberty; privacy of the dwelling of every citizen; a citizen's right to express convictions and opinions freely; the right to assemble peaceably and without arms; the right to form associations and unions; the right to family, education, private property and freedom of religion.

It was decided by Justice Kenny in 1965 that the personal rights which may be invoked to invalidate legislation are not confined to those specified in Article 40 but include all those rights which 'result from the Christian and democratic nature of the State'. Since this ruling, a number of unspecified rights have been recognised and enforced. These include:

- the right to dispose of and withdraw one's labour;
- the right not to belong to a trade union;
- the right to earn one's livelihood;
- the right to work;
- the right to litigate claims;
- the right to prepare for and follow a chosen career;
- the right to consult with, and be represented by, a lawyer when charged with a serious criminal offence;
- the right to be assisted by the State if one's health is in jeopardy,
- the right to marry; and
- the right to free movement within the State.

The Constitution has been developed by interpretation and implied rights. It has been expanded also from hitherto unused sections of the document itself. Thus, for instance, the Preamble, which was previously thought to be of little significance, has been used to keep the Constitution, and the law flowing from it, in touch with prevailing ideas.

The Preamble to the Constitution notes that the people are 'seeking to promote the common good, with due observance of Prudence, Justice and Charity, so that the dignity and freedom of the individual may be assured, true social order attained, the unity of our country restored, and concord established with other nations'.

Ireland and European law

One of the most significant influences on the development of the Irish legal system has been the European Community. The Irish system has had some difficulty reconciling itself with that of the Community. In particular, the Irish Constitution, as a product of Ireland's historical experience, emphasised the notion of sovereignty. An amendment to the Constitution was, therefore, necessary to enable the Republic to become a full member of the EC. The amendment, approved by a large majority, is restricted to approving the existing European Community's arrangements. In December 1985 the Community adopted the Single European Act (SEA) to speed up and make more democratic its decision-making process. To be implemented, the SEA needed to be ratified by all twelve national parliaments. In Ireland, there was a successful court challenge to the SEA on the grounds that it was unconstitutional. The Supreme Court considered that Title 111 of the SEA represented a surrender of sovereignty and exceeded the normal power of governments to conclude international agreements. The Tenth Amendment, passed in 1987, allowed Ireland to ratify the SEA.

European Community law applies directly in member-states to governments, companies and individuals. Its obligations or the rights it establishes must be upheld by national courts and then by the European Court of Justice. The European Community, in effect, makes laws for Irish citizens even though they have not been passed by the Oireachtas. Irish ministers and MEPs are, of course, involved in the process of law-making at the EC level. There are five ways in which EC law changes or influences Irish law. The Council of Ministers and/ or the European Commission can issue regulations, directives, decisions. recommendations and opinions. Regulations have direct effect in Ireland and require little or no domestic action. Directives are binding and may require a change in (a) administrative practice, (b) secondary legislation in the form of ministerial orders called 'statutory instruments' or (c) amended or new legislation. Decisions from the Council and Commission are directly applicable and binding on the government, company or individual to whom they are addressed. The rest – recommendations and opinions – are not legally binding, though they may be considered politically so. Irish courts are not permitted to review EC statutes or their compatibility with the Constitution. A great deal of domestic legislation is now a result of obligations placed on Ireland to conform with EC directives. The supervision of EC law has not been satisfactory. The Joint Oireachtas Committee on the Secondary Legislation of the European Communities has some powers to recommend rejection of ministerial orders consequent on EC directives, but its reports are usually brief and after the event. Debate on European Community law has tended to be perfunctory.

Council of Europe: The European Court of Human Rights

A further profound development in Ireland's legal system is the impact of the European Convention of Human Rights. Under the Convention an aggrieved citizen who has exhausted all domestic remedies may petition the European Commission on Human Rights on the grounds that a state has violated the rights guaranteed in the Convention. The Convention includes an optional provision under which decisions made by the European Court of Human Rights are legally binding in Ireland. Only a constitutional provision cannot be challenged in the European Court. This court, based in Strasbourg, should not be confused with the European Court of Justice (ECJ) in Luxembourg. The ECJ is a European Community institution, while the European Court of Human Rights was set up by the Council of Europe which consists of twenty-one West European parliamentary democracies. All EC member-states recognise the jurisdiction of the Court in Strasbourg in human rights cases.

The first major direct influence the European Court of Human Rights had on the Irish system of justice was to establish that a

petitioner must be able to seek redress before national courts. A
form of legal aid provision in civil cases has had to be introduced
in the Republic in response to a decision of the European Court
that, in a particular case, the expense of legal proceedings put
them outside an individual's reach.

As stated above, a constitution is supposed to reflect and codify
the values and beliefs of its society. Values in Ireland are
frequently different from those elsewhere in Europe. In matters of
individual rights, laws in most European countries are more liberal
than Irish law. A significant number of people in both Northern
Ireland and the Republic fear the changes which decisions of the
European Court of Human Rights may have in Ireland. Probably
the first important decision to highlight this problem was in 1981,
when a case was brought by Geoffrey Dudgeon before the courts
in Northern Ireland on the basis of the judgement of the European
Court of Human Rights that homosexual activity between con-
senting adults should be permitted. Although the case was lost on
a technicality, it reinforced the image of the European Court. The
basis of Dudgeon's claim was that current law violated a guaranteed right to privacy. The case increased the fears of those wishing
to retain Ireland less liberal laws that they might be changed from
outside. This fear was clearly demonstrated in the campaign for
the Eighth Amendment (see below). In 1988, the European Court
of Human Rights again showed its importance for Ireland by
upholding the claim of David Norris that his rights were infringed
by the criminal law on homosexuality. As a result of the Norris
case, the Irish government will almost certainly have to introduce
new legislation to replace the existing laws of 1861 and 1865 on
homosexual acts, just as Northern Irish law had to be changed
after Dudgeon.

The Eighth Amendment

From 1981 until 1983 one of the most divisive debates in the
Republic of Ireland surrounded the eventually successful campaign for the Eighth Amendment to the Constitution to protect
the life of the 'unborn'. Abortion seemed to be prevented quite

adequately by an 1861 Act. The overwhelming majority of those campaigning against the Amendment were at pains to point out that they did *not* want to see abortion introduced. They were against the Eighth Amendment because they saw it as unnecessary and divisive. The campaign can be understood, however, in terms of the fear that judicial interpretation either in Ireland or at the European Court of Human Rights might change the law.

Another constitutional amendment campaign to delete the article which declares that 'no law shall be enacted providing for the grant of a dissolution of marriage' (41.3.2) was fought in 1986. Those in favour of provision for divorce in Ireland used two legal weapons. Firstly, they attempted to convince the electorate at the referendum that the deletion of the article was necessary. Secondly, a case was taken to the European Court of Human Rights by an Irish couple to test whether Irish law on divorce contravened their rights and those of their daughter. Despite the fact that both the court case and referendum failed, it demonstrates that Irish people are willing to use the European Courts of Human Rights for legal redress.

The effects of the situation in Northern Ireland

The outbreak of civil unrest in Northern Ireland in the 1960s brought the 'national question' back on to the agenda in the Republic. Bunreacht na hEireann claims the whole island of Ireland as being the national territory (Article 2), but also accepts that 'the right of the Parliament and Government established by this Constitution to exercise jurisdiction over the whole of that territory' would be restricted to the twenty-six counties of the country (Article 3). Bunreacht na hEireann was also imbued with a Catholic ethos, even recognising the special position of that Church as the faith of the vast majority of the population (Article 44). For these reasons it was not a constitution likely to appeal to unionists or Protestants.

As we have already seen, Ireland was undergoing major changes in the 1960s. The replacement of de Valera by Seán Lemass marked this change. The new Taoiseach sought to modernise and update Ireland's institutions. He argued that the Constitution needed to be reviewed. In 1966 the three main political parties agreed to take part in an informal committee 'to review constitutional, legislative and institutional bases of government'. Its report in December 1967 came up with twenty-seven areas which it believed could be open to change. The Fianna Fáil government eventually decided to pursue a change in the electoral system, which the other members of the Committee did not wish to see. The cross-party approach to constitutional reform was seriously damaged.

Article 44 and the Unionists of Northern Ireland

As a result of the unrest in the north there was pressure to have some form of positive action by the Irish government to eliminate Protestant fears. The only section of the Constitution on which there was both cross-party and wide social support for change was Article 44. Article 44.1.2 recognised 'the special position of the Holy Catholic Apostolic and Roman Church as the guardian of the faith professed by the great majority of the citizens'. Its removal was accepted in a referendum in 1972. It was argued that, as it gave no rights or advantages to the Catholic Church and had negative connotations for Protestants, it was as well removed.

Although Northern Ireland's problems brought constitutional review to the fore, there was no consensus in the Republic on sensitive issue such as Articles 2 and 3. There has, therefore, been some reluctance by the political parties to bring forward suggestions for constitutional change. The parties' attitudes to the Constitution has become linked to their policies on Northern Ireland. Fine Gael and Labour argue that the way forward is to take out the offending pieces of the Constitution, as a sign of goodwill. Fianna Fáil want change only when representatives from both the Republic and Northern Ireland sit down to discuss the future of the whole country.

The most forthright advocates for constitutional change are the Progressive Democrats. In January 1988 they produced a blueprint for an entirely new constitution. The party acknowledged their debt to the former Fine Gael leader, Garret FitzGerald, who as Taoiseach in 1981–82 launched what has become known as the 'Constitutional Crusade'. The aim of the Crusade was to remove those articles from the Constitution which were objectionable to unionists and Protestants. Fianna Fáil opposed the Crusade and no agreed general review was undertaken. The Progressive Democrats, however, feel that the Anglo–Irish Agreement of 1985 should encourage a new attempt. In line with the tone of the Agreement, which will be outlined in Chapter 7, they propose that Articles 2 and 3 of the Constitution be deleted. Further, a completely new constitution should be introduced. The new document would reaffirm Ireland's aspiration to unity but acknowledge that it can only be achieved with majority consent in Northern Ireland. Further, the Progressive Democrat 'constitution' allows for a clear separation of church and state and the legal possibility of divorce.

Conclusions

Bunreacht na hEireann is, like all constitutions, bound by the ideological concerns, political dangers and aspirations of its authors. Over fifty years later some of its provisions appear less well-founded than de Valera, its principle progenitor, hoped. Some of its novel features, such as the vocational second chamber, have developed quite differently than expected. Today attitudes to such areas as the role of women and relations with Northern Ireland are in sharp contrast to those which shaped the document itself. Nevertheless, the Constitution as amended, interpreted and informally augmented by politicians, civil servants and judges remains a central document for Irish politics today. As a working set of rules and principles, it is the focus of debate about new social and political rights and obligations. Alterations to it are one important measure of the pace of social and political change.

Further reading

B. Chubb, *Sourcebook of Irish Government*, Dublin: Institute of

Public Administration, 1983.

B. Doolan, *Constitutional Law and Constitutional Rights in Ireland*, Dublin: Gill & Macmillan, 1984.

B. Farrell, *De Valera's Constitution and Ours,* Dublin: Gill & Macmillan, 1988.

6
LOCAL GOVERNMENT

Local government is less powerful and provides less services in Ireland than in most other European countries. There is no recent tradition of local autonomy and no legal basis for local authorities to broaden their functions beyond those which central government gives them. At the moment the list is dominated by housing, roads, water supply, sanitary services, development control and environmental protection. It is likely that this latter area will become even more significant as public concern with the environment puts pressure on central government. Similarly in some authorities, libraries and swimming pools may be the focus of increased public demand. On the other hand, some tasks, such as vehicle licensing, now with local government, may be removed, as was the provision of health services some years ago. For example, the government set up the National Roads Authority with responsibility for the network of national roads. This obviously reduces the role of local authorities in relation to roads generally. So the term 'local government' encompasses a varying collection of tasks, even including the upkeep of courthouses, the dipping of sheep against scabs, the issuing and collection of dog licences under the Animals Act 1988 and the rehabilitation of itinerants. The local authorities themselves, however, have proved enduring and they remain an important part of Irish democracy.

Local government in Ireland is based upon nineteenth-century British legislation which basically provided for single-tier urban and two-tier rural government. The services it provides are broadly similar to its British equivalent without responsibility for

Table 6.1 *Major responsibilities of non-metropolitan county councils in England and county and county borough councils in Ireland*

	England	Ireland
Consumer protection	✓	
Education	✓	✓[1]
Fire service	✓	✓
Police	✓	
Housing		✓
Libraries	✓	✓
Museums and art galleries	✓	✓
Parks and recreation	✓	✓
Personal social services	✓	
Refuse collection		✓
Refuse disposal	✓	✓
Sewerage (local servicing)		✓
Town and county planning	✓	✓
Roads	✓	✓
Transport	✓	
Youth employment	✓	
Drainage		✓
Water supply		✓
Environmental protection		✓

Note: [1] = Vocational education only through semi-autonomous Vocational Education Committees.

education, the police and many social services (see Table 6.1). The chief Irish innovations have involved the establishment of a national agency for local government appointments (1926), a concentration of administrative powers in the office of city/county manager (1940) and the 'abolition' of the domestic rating system (1978). The major Irish legislation is, in effect, nineteenth-century British statutes with a time lag, e.g. the 1834 (British) and 1838 (Irish) Poor Law reforms, the 1835 (British) and 1840 (Irish) Municipal Corporations Acts and 1888 (British) and the 1898 (Irish) Local Government Acts.

The five major urban authorities, formally called 'county

Table 6.2 *First preference votes in selected local, Dáil and European elections 1979–91 (%)*

Party	Election						
	Local 1979	European 1984	Local 1985	Dáil 1987	Dáil 1989	European 1989	Local 1991
Fianna Fáil	39	39	46	44	44	32	38
Fine Gael	35	32	30	27	29	22	27
Labour	12	8	8	6	10	10	11
Others	14	20	16	22	17	36	24

Source: Department of the Environment Reports.

Table 6.3 *Percentage of seats gained in 1979, 1985 and 1991 county and county borough elections*

Party	1979	1985	1991
Fianna Fáil	43	49	41
Fine Gael	39	32	31
Labour	10	7	10
Prog. Democrats	–	–	4
Others	8	12	14
	100	100	100
Total no. of seats	806	833	883

Source: Department of the Environment Reports.

boroughs', cover the larger cities, Dublin, Cork, Limerick, Waterford and, a recent addition, Galway. The rest of the country is divided into twenty-seven county council areas, some of which have subordinate authorities within them, known as urban districts and town commissioners. Each local authority comprises two elements – the elected members (councillors) and a manager. County boroughs have between fifteen and fifty-two members; outside Dublin the number ranges from twenty to forty-eight.

Table 6.4 *Control of councils in 1979, 1985 and 1991*

Dominant party	Percentage of councils		
	1979*	*1985**	*1991*
Fianna Fáil	10	55	15
Fine Gael	3	0	0
Fine Gael/Labour	45	6	N/A
No overall majority	42	39	85
*Based on Dublin County as one council			

Source: Department of the Environment Reports.

Local government elections are held infrequently. At the 1991 elections Fianna Fáil gained almost 41 per cent of the seats – a big decline compared with their previous performance in 1985. Local elections use the single transferable vote (STV) system in multi-member constituencies. A recurring election theme is the financing of local government, especially the level of water and other service charges.

Turnout in the 1991 elections was 55 per cent compared to 57 per cent in 1985. It was generally highest in rural and western areas. Turnout was 43 per cent in Dublin and 52 per cent in Cork. The low turnout in Dublin and the importance of local issues means that these elections are not a reliable guide to national trends, and the impact on the national party system is not likely to be great. The competition for seats is partisan but there is a great emphasis on local loyalties and personal service by councillors.

Fianna Fáil's share of the local vote at 38 per cent was 8 per cent down on their 1985 performance. Government supporters regarded this result as a return to their usual local government levels and pointed to 1979. Fine Gael were also satisfied that their vote represented a halt to a recent run of poor results (see Table 6.2). Party fortunes are also reflected in seats won (see Table 6.3).

Almost all councillors in Ireland are elected formally or implicitly under the banner of a political party. While no council is dominated by forces other than Fianna Fáil or Fine Gael (either independently or in an arrangement with independents and smaller parties), the 1991 elections substantially decreased the hold of Fianna Fáil. Table 6.4 shows the party situation in terms of councils won in 1979, 1985 and 1991.

Of the minor parties, the 1991 election was most significant for the Progressive Democrats, who were contesting in local elections for the first time. The PD share of the vote was just below their general election tally but many more seats were won. Similarly, Labour made substantial gains in terms of seats won.

The managerial system

The institution of city or county manager is the most distinctive and innovative feature of Irish local government. Broadly the manager replaced the executive committees of the British system. He 'reports' his decisions to the council; its ability to overturn them is limited but, as will be shown below, controversial. The management system was constructed by the revolutionary elite after independence in order to bring about efficient and honest local administration. The period of civil turmoil leading up to 1922 had seen a decline in standards of administration and accounting. The first Irish governments acted quickly and resolutely to stamp out malpractice. Appointments procedure, auditing and other administrative practices were reformed and public confidence in local government was restored.

The management system was devised as a result of public satisfaction with the role of the commissioners who had replaced those local authorities suspended by the first governments. The management system was first tried in the cities of Cork, Dublin and Limerick. By 1942, it was in place throughout Ireland. The managers have become accepted as above suspicion and the public image of local government has improved, reflecting their contribution to Irish life.

By the 1960s Seán Lemass recognised that local authorities had an expanded role to play in national development. He talked of local authorities as 'development corporations'. Most managers have sought to fulfil this role despite legal and financial restrictions. The managers have offered leadership in policy formulation and direction. The contribution of elected politicians has been to legitimise that leadership and to facilitate the execution of policy by intervening on behalf of aggrieved citizens.

Irish civil servants and ministers talk of local democracy but in practice have sought to hold a tight rein on local authorities. This tendency is accentuated by the current economic and fiscal crises. Governments have sought recently to increase the amount of locally raised revenue. Local government finances are drawn from state grants, charges for services and the rates, a local property tax. The proportion of GNP accounted for by local spending had risen by the late 1970s to 17 per cent compared to 10 per cent of a much smaller GNP in 1939.

In 1977, the Fianna Fáil election manifesto promised to abolish rates on private homes. This pledge was a major part of the party's election strategy. The rates promise was fulfilled after Jack Lynch's landslide victory, by the Local Government (Financial Provisions) Act 1978. Thus, central government undertook to reimburse local authorities for all the loss of rate income on dwellings and certain other properties including secondary schools and community halls. Rates on business properties remained, though they represented a small proportion of the total locally-generated income. Crucially, the 1978 Act also gave the Minister for the Environment a power of limitation with regard to local authority finance. The Minister was able to set the maximum rate increase. The central government wished to prevent 'local authorities from increasing rates indiscriminately'. Councils retained the power to set the rate level but, with the Minister's control of the maximum, the financial independence of local government has been drastically curtailed.

The loss of the rates as a truly independent local tax had a particularly marked affect on local government. The most visible symbol of local autonomy, setting the rate level, was in effect removed. The increased dependency of local authorities on the state for revenue income from 1978 onwards is shown by Table 6.5. The financial independence of local government has been drastically curtailed. The rate level has become an instrument of central government economic management and, consequently, has been held well below inflation, as Table 6.6 shows.

Table 6.5 *Local authority finance, 1970–83 (IR£m)*

	Revenue	Capital	Total	Rates as % of revenue
1970	158	37	195	32
1972	131	50	181	46
1977	317	145	462	35
1982	803	415	1,218	15
1983	900	450	1,350	11

Between 1978 and 1981 local authorities adjusted to the new regime of high inflation and decreasing income by reducing the level of services. The shortfall was also met by running down reserves. The impact varied according to the levels of rates in 1977 and the reserves of each authority. There is no mechanism for rate equalisation. Some authorities, especially in areas of urban and suburban growth, enjoyed a degree of rate buoyancy from new developments. On the whole, however, the effect on local government was general cutbacks, restrictions and retrenchment. The system suffered a corresponding decrease in morale, public image and effectiveness.

Table 6.6 *Rate level increases as compared to inflation, 1978–82 (%)*

	1978	1979	1980	1981	1982	Simple total
Rate limit	11	10	10	12	15	58
Average inflation	7.6	13.2	18.2	20.4	17.4	77

Source: R. Paddison & S. Bailey (eds.), *Local Government Finance*, Routledge, 1988, p. 222.

The 1982 circular on rates introduced a new element to local government finance. While notifying a 15 per cent increase in permitted maximum rate levels it also announced a shortfall in the grant. The government in effect was putting up only 92 per cent of the actual figures required. The gap was to be made up by each authority by charges though the statute authorising these were not in place. The Minister promised to introduce the appropriate legislation 'at an early date' aimed at (a) providing for a scale of fees for planning applications and (b) giving local authorities a general power to charge for local services. The idea of charges as a relief to local taxation had been mooted as far back as the 1960s but its introduction in 1982 was unexpected.

The aims of central government in relation to fiscal and monetary policies have little to do with individual local authority needs. Nevertheless, having found itself in a fiscal crisis in the 1980s as a result of its narrow base of direct taxation and high foreign debt repayments, the central government has sought to shift a greater proportion of its burden on to local government. Central funding now falls short of local authority spending so charges for local services have to make up the difference. Thus, the local authorities are in effect acting as tax gatherers for central government – incurring the odium of the public but unable to improve their overall income sufficiently despite imposing more extensive charges for services. Water charges have been particularly unpopular and difficult to collect. Local residents often resent what they see as rates in a new guise. Central government has, therefore, used local government as a means of deflecting criticism, raising finance and reducing public expenditure.

Governments have recently come to recognise the need to break the cycle of retrenchment in services and increases in prices. The introduction of a general property tax as a means of financing local authorities and reducing their dependence on the central exchequer would, however, be very difficult to introduce because of its electoral unpopularity.

After independence, the new government took a series of measures to assert central authority in areas of local government remuneration and recruitment. A central recruitment agency was formed to appoint local public servants. This agency, the Local Appointments Commission (LAC), still exists and, in effect, removes any local discretion in the hiring and firing of local officials. The LAC was a major departure from British practice, which had previously been followed, with each local authority being responsible for its own staff. Thus, Irish local government officers do not depend on councillors for appointment or promotion. This gives the local bureaucrats, particularly, of course, the

manager, a significant degree of independence from the pressure
of elected members in their councils.

The local politician's role in local affairs is predominantly to
offer himself as an intermediary between constituents and the
broad range of state bureaucracy. Local government is likely to be
only one of his concerns. For the most part, Irish politicians are
'local politicians', however high they climb in the elected hierarchy. Most TDs are also councillors. Very few deputies, except
ministers and their shadows, ever have to broaden their consideration of the purposes of local authorities beyond that of sources
of individual benefits and electoral advantage. In practice, the
current *modus operandi*, under which policy initiatives remain with
the manager, suits the politicians. Too close an association with
controversial general policies would endanger their brokerage
power base. At the same time most managers are able to accommodate the needs of politicians for 'apparent' influence without
seriously compromising general policy.

The only major exceptions to the established understanding
between politicians and manager arise in relation to planning
controls. Councillors in some authorities make regular use of their
residual power to overturn a manager's decision as it applies to a
particular individual. This power is generally described with
reference to its statutory basis in section 4 of the County
Management Act 1955. A 'section four' motion, if passed, permits
a council to direct the manager to act in a specific instance in a
particular way. Typically, it allows planning permission to an
individual where general criteria would indicate refusal. Often
such cases concern the building of individual houses outside the
general terms of the development plan for the area. About half of
all newly-built private houses in Ireland are now 'one-off' homes,
many built in spite of planning and other public consideration. In
several counties this contravention of planning rules is regularly
achieved through the use of 'section fours'. Their usefulness in the
clientelist system has made 'section fours' very valuable political
assets. Unlike other state benefits like houses and roads, planning
permissions 'cost' councils nothing and are in unlimited supply.
Once a council has established a pattern of section four

permissions, however, it is difficult to stop granting them because refusal becomes politically costly.

The other major display of councillor power comes with the adoption and adaptation of the development plan. Each major council is the planning authority for its area and as such is legally obliged to draw up a development plan indicating the pattern of land use. Thus the development plan divides the county or city into zones in which residential, agricultural, industrial or other activities will predominate. Planning applications are allowed or refused with reference to the development plan. The commercial value of land is markedly influenced by the category into which it is zoned. The pressure on politicians to assert their legal rights can be very great.

The position the manager holds in relation to the elected representatives of his area is a by-product of political competition. There are few rewards for the politician in competing with the manager for control over most areas of policy. Nor does the public put pressures on councillors to fight on a broad policy front. Pressure-group activity involving local government has until recently been very limited, particularly outside Dublin. The major national pressure groups, especially those representing farming and business, are organised at a sub-national level but they rarely operate through county or city councillors. On local government issues, the major interest groups will generally communicate with the appropriate officials directly, or in counties especially, through the manager. Cultural, social and sporting groups rarely exert pressure on local government at the level of broad policy. There is a virtual consensus in Ireland on housing and welfare provision which is only strained significantly for local authorities in relation to itinerant settlement.

Pressure-groups' activity in Irish local government is largely confined to detailed and specific provisions such as road improvements or refuse collection. On these issues residents' associations or *ad hoc* groups may solicit the support of local politicians. Such pressure may cause a particular decision to be reviewed. The exception to this particularistic, low-key pressure-group activity concerns major planning applications, such as the siting of gas or oil storage facilities or the nationally-organised campaigns against charges for services. In both cases the issues involved ultimately transcend the local arena and the crucial decisions are made at the national level. Most councillors only become involved when the pressure group's request is local, specific, achievable in the short term and open to favourable publicity. Further, councillors may wish to avoid association with issues that too obviously divide the local electorate. In the event of a councillor coming under local pressure, he or she may well be pleased that the manager will publicly accept responsibility for unpopular decisions. Pressure-group activity is greatest in urban areas. New housing developments quickly form residents' associations. Councillors try to avoid these becoming alternative sources of complaint, and thus politicians become involved with such groups early.

In some urban areas, particularly those with a strong republican tradition, local political activists are using residents' associations to challenge the hegemony of the more established political parties. Again councillors, TDs and their supporters see this development as a challenge and respond by seeking to enhance their own ability to respond to 'client groups'. Thus a number of advice centres associated with particular parties or politicians have been opened in several urban areas in Dublin and elsewhere. Some of these offices are well equipped with word processors, automatic answering machines and duplicating machines. Their aim, however, is to provide the traditional politician's services more efficiently.

'Parish pump' politics in Ireland have received a lot of academic interest. Some writers have predicted their demise as Ireland experiences the pressures of modernisation. Irish society in general has become more urban and, economically, has moved away from its agrarian base. The greater Dublin area now contains about one-third of the population. Though many of the political and social attitudes of its citizens are shared with Irish people generally, Dublin has a more mobile and complex class structure. The needs of its inhabitants are likely to become more distinctive.

Organisationally, Dublin local authorities are more complex, pressure group attention more intense and consensus on policy more difficult to achieve. The management function in Dublin is carried out by a team of assistant managers, of which the city and county manager is the head. The three current Dublin authorities employ over 4,500 people in officer grades and they are dispersed widely over the area. The problems of development in Ireland generally are likely to increase in the near future for very predictable reasons – the demographic and geographic imbalance of the population and economic underachievement relative to its European partners and emergent Third World competitors. The staff of Dublin local authorities will be hard-pressed to cope with the consequences. Already, Dublin's development problems are mirrored by typical indicators of social malaise such as drug abuse and crime.

Population of the Republic

The population of the Republic of Ireland on the night of 5 April 1981 was 3.4 million nearly half of whom were aged under 25 years. The population for the same area in 1841 was around 6.5 million. Life expectancy in 1981 was 69 years for males and 73 for females. The estimated population in 1990 was 3.5.million.

Faced with increasing pressure in Dublin, the national government's response has been pragmatic and piecemeal. In 1985 a new structure for local government in metropolitan Dublin was outlined. Under the Local Government (Reorganisation) Act 1985, Dublin was due to be controlled by four authorities, three 'counties' and the existing county borough. This legislation was left inoperative until after the 1991 election.

The changes in Dublin may be leading to further reform. If so, among the most likely is the establishment of more authorities below the level of county and county borough. Currently there is a very wide range of councillor/population and councillor/area ratios around the country (see Table 6.7). If new forms of elected

Table 6.7 *Ratio of councillors to population and area in selected local authorities*

Authority	Population	Area (sq. m.)
Dublin CC	1:10,500	1: 8.4
Dublin CB	1:10,500	1: 1.1
New Dublin CCs	1: 6,119	—
Cork CC	1: 5,544	1:62.5
Cork CB	1: 4,260	1: 0.5
Limerick CC	1: 3,604	1:38.4
Limerick CB	1: 4,049	1: 0.4
Waterford CC	1: 2,179	1:30.9
Waterford CB	1: 2,565	1: 0.2
Mayo CC	1: 3,702	1:69.6
Leitrim CC	1: 1,300	1:27.9

Sources: Administration Yearbook and Diary and *Irish Times*, 18 June 1985.

authority are created, then it is likely that aspects of the recreation and other amenity services could be devolved to them. Already, many local authorities are experimenting with local area committees and decentralised offices. At the same time, however, several non-elected local government bodies, such as county development teams and county committees of agriculture, have been abolished.

Another possible reform is the strengthening of the institution of Lord Mayor or Chairman of the council. Currently these posts are largely ceremonial and filled annually by election within the council. A recent Lord Mayor of Dublin has suggested a directly-elected mayor standing on a city-wide basis for a period of years. Such a democratically responsible official could more easily resist the pressures of local councillors. The new mayor or chairperson would complement the leadership role of the manager. He or she would help the formulation and implementation of difficult policies. The publicly acclaimed success of Lord Mayor Carmencita Hederman as the 'first citizen' of the city during the Dublin millennium celebrations of 1988 has greatly enhanced the prestige of the post. The time may now be right for a change in the respective roles of bureaucrat and politician in Irish local government.

Regions

The attitude of central government to local government is heavily influenced by the idea that Ireland already has too many elected local authorities and members. Critics of this view point to the lack of comparative international evidence but officials in the Department of the Environment seem firmly convinced of the need for reductions in the number of councils and councillors. Had Ireland gone through the kind of radical overhaul of local government common in other European countries in recent decades, there would probably be more rather than less local government.

Changes at European Community level have brought about changes in local government structures. In August 1988, the Minister for Finance announced new arrangements for responding to a commitment from the European Commission to aid the least prosperous EC regions, provided satisfactory plans and programmes were submitted for the Structural Fund, which is due to be doubled by 1992. The new regime for the Fund came into operation in January 1989 and for the purpose of giving maximum advantage for Ireland the country has been divided into seven regions. These regions do not relate directly to the functional division of the country for health, energy or other service purposes. They will involve elected representatives only indirectly. The primary purpose of the regional structure is to satisfy the European Commission, which favours sub-national government for Structural Fund purposes, and to facilitate consultation with local interests.

Conclusions

Local government in Ireland, as an independent, adequately resourced and innovative part of the nation's life, has been on the decline since the 1970s. The keys to its reduced role are in the lack of sufficient truly local revenue, the neglect of its long-term future by central government and the public indifference to local democracy.

In 1991, however, a committee of experts reported to the government that major changes should be made. It called for a system of regional, county and district local authorities. The commitee proposed eight statutory regional authorities to promote public service co-ordination at regional level. Outside Dublin, county and city boundaries should remain largely unchanged but more responsibilities should be given to the councils. In the Dublin area, the city should retain its existing boundaries; Dún Laoghaire should be extended and upgraded to city status; and the balance of the County Dublin area divided into two new county authorities. Dublin City and each of these new authorities should have their own city or county manager. The committee argued that there are serious defects in the current urban district arrangements and these are in need of fundamental overhaul. From the initial political reaction, it seems that new district councils covering the whole country will be set up. Legislature facilitating the new arrangements in Dublin was prepared after the 1991 local elections. Many of the committee's other recommendations are also likely to find legislative expression in the next few years and local government may come to play a more vital role in Irish politics.

Further reading

N. Collins, *Local Government Managers at Work*, Dublin: Institute of Public Administration, 1987.

D. Roche, *Local Government in Ireland*, Dublin: Institute of Public Administration, 1982.

7
NORTHERN IRELAND

As a distinct political entity, Northern Ireland came into being in 1921 under the Government of Ireland Act 1920 (see Chapter 1). This Act created two Irish states: 'Northern Ireland', consisting of the six north-eastern counties, and `Southern Ireland', consisting of the rest of the country. Separate parliaments were planned but the plan became effective immediately only for Northern Ireland. When the Irish Free State gained independence in 1922, Northern Ireland continued its union with Britain. The Unionist Party took over the reins of power and enjoyed fifty years of uninterrupted one-party rule until the abolition of the Northern Ireland parliament in 1972. Periodically, political and religious antagonisms in Northern Ireland have flared into civil disorder; in the early 1920s, for example, the IRA mounted a formidable offensive against the new regime. On the whole, however, the government of Northern Ireland retained firm control until the late 1960s. Since 1968 there has been a major escalation of violence which has claimed over 2,700 lives, both military and civilian. In addition, over 27,000 people have been injured.

The current 'troubles' were precipitated by the failure of the liberal wing of the governing Unionist Party to persuade their colleagues to concede the full demands of the civil rights movement in 1968–69. These demands, which arose from Catholics' perception of discrimination in employment opportunities and public policy, included a fairer system for the allocation of public housing, local government reforms and fair employment practices. The Northern Ireland government feared that the civil rights protesters were simply the current form of nationalism or republicanism and that the stability of the union with Britain was threatened.[1] Ironically, although the Protestant working class also suffered some of the same disadvantages as the Catholics, they were discouraged from joining the protests. Their leaders claimed that Protestant participation in the protest would be 'treasonable' in assisting the republicans and the cause of a united Ireland. Accordingly, the government deployed their largely Protestant security forces to maintain order and made few concessions to the civil rights protesters. Marches and meetings were broken up and the police were seen to be co-operating closely with Protestant counter-protesters. A serious outbreak of sectarian violence forced the British government to intervene. British troops were deployed in large numbers in 1969 in an attempt to restore order. Northern Ireland's parliament and government were suspended in March 1972. Since then, direct rule from London has been carried on under a UK cabinet minister – the Secretary of State for Northern Ireland.

Religion and political divisions

From the beginning politics in Northern Ireland were dominated by the question of partition. Every election was an occasion for one side to affirm its commitment to the Union and the other to reject it. Discussion of politics is often expressed in religious terms which seem anachronistic to the outsider. It is useful, therefore, before going on to describe Northern Ireland's institutions, to discuss briefly the nature of the division.

The roots of the political divisions in Northern Ireland are set in the differential success of British colonial policy in the island of Ireland. As was discussed in Chapter 3, plantation was the means by which English rule in Ireland was firmly established. An attempt was made to uproot one group of people, the native Catholics, and replace them with Protestant outsiders whose loyalty was assured. The greater success of the policy in the northeast set the province of Ulster apart. The policy of plantation for Ulster began in earnest in 1607 and was largely over by 1641 but it established the current pattern of social and economic division. It is broadly true that there are still two camps though each is itself divided. The division within each community finds imperfect expression in the four largest political parties: the unionist side is represented by the Official Unionist Party (OU) and the Democratic Unionist Party (DUP) while the nationalists have the Social Democratic and Labour Party (SDLP) and Sinn Féin (SF). The political parties are discussed in more detail later. In broad terms, however, the rallying calls of opposing political forces tend not to appeal across the Catholic/Protestant community divide.

The Protestant majority in Northern Ireland is divided into a number of groups but the largest are the Presbyterians and the Church of Ireland. For many Protestants, particularly those who think of themselves as loyalists, Northern Ireland is the last bastion of the true tradition of the Reformation. It stands alone in a world of secularism, communism and Popism: 'Both Romanism and Communism have absorbed the basic elements of pagan philosophy to bolster up their false and anti-God systems'.[2] For the loyalists the link with the British Protestant Crown has been a guarantee of a Protestant hegemony which could not be sustained in a united Irish state. If Britain were to seek to weaken its commitment to Northern Ireland some loyalists would prefer independence to an all-Ireland settlement. Other Protestants, or more correctly unionists, also want to remain British. They have no wish to leave the wider British community with its cultural tradition, liberal–democratic institutions and Commonwealth of nations. The symbols that charge the emotions of unionists include the Monarchy, the Union flag, the Houses of Parliament and other institutions shared with England, Scotland and Wales. A significant number of Unionists are in favour of fully integrating Northern Ireland with Britain.

The Catholic community forms roughly 40 per cent of the population of Northern Ireland. It is, like the Protestant community, divided by class and other social distinctions. The SDLP, for example, enjoys a higher level of support among the middle class than does Sinn Féin. Catholics are united, however, by mistrust of the Protestants and antipathy to Britain. Although they have suffered sustained and systematic disadvantage, not all Catholics are economically marginal and socially deprived. On the other hand, whether rich or poor, the Catholic community is socially distinct. For many in both the Catholic and Protestant communities contact with the other side is largely perfunctory.

Much of Catholic social life is organised separately from the Protestants. Significantly, Catholic children attend schools run under the auspices of the Church. The ethos in these schools is clearly denominational and Irish in outlook. Many schools are controlled by religious orders. The UK government supports Catholic schools by meeting their full running costs and contributing 85 per cent of capital investment. The state schools are in effect Protestant and reflect a self-consciously British outlook. Recent legislative changes requiring all schools to teach the topics of Education for Mutual Understanding and Cultural Heritage may lead to a shift in perspectives. The UK government has also shown some enthusiasm for integrated education.

Part of the sectarian strategy of governments in Belfast after 1922 was to exclude Catholics from certain areas of the economy. The Unionist government of Northern Ireland identified its central task as protecting Protestant interests. In 1934 the Prime Minister, Sir James Craig, told the lower chamber of the Northern Ireland legislature: 'all I boast is that we are a Protestant Parliament and a Protestant State'.[3]

Catholics form a larger proportion of the population in the west than in the east of Northern Ireland. The uneven development of capitalism in Ireland has left much of this area relatively underdeveloped. Government economic development schemes did operate but many Catholics contend that, to preserve the Protestant dominance, employment opportunities were kept from Catholic areas. It is pointed out that in 1971, for example, Catholic unemployment was 13.9 per cent and the Protestant figure was 5.6 per cent. Catholics were more likely to be found in occupations which experienced the highest rates of seasonal and long-term unemployment. Economic decline, fair employment legislation and the increased impact of multinational businesses may be redressing this imbalance. The major locally-owned businesses remain, however, essentially Protestant. Catholic employment is significantly higher in the public sector. The Catholic middle classes are found disproportionately in the liberal professions where entry is largely determined by educational achievement.

The physically most obvious aspect of the distinctly Catholic experience in Northern Ireland is segregated housing. For reasons of electoral advantage and social control, public housing was for a long time allocated on sectarian lines. Northern Ireland had the worst housing conditions in the UK. Agitation by civil rights campaigners in the later 1960s resulted in the removal of control of housing from the local authorities. Since the outbreak of violence and despite very much improved housing conditions, the segregation of housing on sectarian lines has increased as members of each community seek safety in numbers.

Parties and elections in Northern Ireland

The fundamental issue at all Northern Irish elections is the relationship been the two parts of Ireland. Since 1922, the status of Northern Ireland within the UK has dominated Ulster politics. The UK general election of 1987 illustrates the pattern of most recent contests with some current issue or government policy being used as a stalking-horse for the basic constitutional issue.

In 1987 the Unionists, who support the present link with Britain, focused their attention on the Anglo–Irish Agreement. As will be outlined in more detail below, in this treaty, signed in November 1985, the Irish and UK governments affirm that any change in the status of Northern Ireland would only come about with the consent of a majority of its people. The Republic recognised that Northern Ireland will remain part of the UK until a majority formally consent to a united Ireland. The Agreement does, however, give the Republic's government a consultative role in several aspects of policy formulation in Northern Ireland. In the general election and subsequent local government by-elections, the Unionist parties, Official Unionist and Democratic Unionists presented a united front in opposition to the Agreement by agreeing not to oppose each other. The DUP had been formed in

1971 by the Revd Ian Paisley and others because the OU was seen as insufficiently resolute in defending unionist interests, but the two parties now co-operate very closely.

The nationalist parties, that is those seeking political change in an all-Ireland context, are divided on the Anglo-Irish Agreement. The Social Democratic and Labour Party support it, but Sinn Féin (SF) opposes the Agreement. SF calls for a clear commitment from the UK government to a united Ireland. For SF the terrorism of the Provisional IRA is a legitimate part of the nationalist campaign. The SDLP favours peaceful and constitutional change and opposes the violent tactics of all paramilitary forces.

Elections in Northern Ireland are largely contests within each tradition. Very few voters move between the Nationalist and Unionist camps. There are, however, several parties which attempt to offer alternatives. The most significant are: (a) the Alliance Party, a cross-community grouping which favours the union while welcoming the Agreement and calling for new Northern Irish institutions; and (b) the Workers' Party, which calls for a united socialist Ireland but stresses class issues above all. Most of the seventeen seats in the UK parliament which are allocated to Northern Ireland are safe for the incumbent. In 1987, only one seat changed hands. Elections do, however, point to the state of public opinion as reflected in the share of the vote which each party gains.

The Unionist vote in 1987 was 49.5 per cent, down 4.5 per cent compared with the 1983 general election. Obviously the fact that competition for Unionist voters was muted by the agreement between the OU and the DUP had a depressing effect. The relative support of the two Unionist parties is difficult to assess because of their pact. Nevertheless, the OU is clearly the larger party and, in terms of general election support, its advantage increased in 1987, gaining 37.8 per cent of the total vote compared to 11.7 per cent for the DUP. The Alliance and Workers' Parties both improved their share of the vote to 10 per cent and 2.6 per cent respectively, but took no seats and each lost several deposits.

On the nationalist side the main contest was between the

SDLP and SF. The 'swing' of between 2 and 3 per cent compared to 1983 favoured the SDLP and the party gained one extra seat. Support among nationalists for the party opposed to the Anglo-Irish Agreement and in favour of the Provisional IRA is still substantial. Overall SF received 25.1 per cent of the nationalist vote and the SDLP 64.9 per cent.

The Northern Ireland economy

Northern Ireland has been described as a caricature of a 'dependent economy', dependent on external funding, external ideas and external initiatives.[4] Dependence on British government aid is a characteristic of many Northern Ireland companies as it is for the economy as a whole. The public sector accounts for roughly 45 per cent of those in employment.[5] Such dependence on public funding led Rowthorn to describe Northern Ireland as

a vast workhouse, in which most of the inmates are engaged in servicing or controlling each other ... it (Northern Ireland) imports a great deal from the outside world whilst providing few exports in return, moreover, as in the case of a workhouse or prison, the gap between imports and exports is financed out of taxes levied on the external population.[6]

The seasonally adjusted unemployment rate in February 1991 was 6.8 per cent for Great Britain and 13.5 per cent in Northern Ireland. Areas such as West Belfast, Derry and Strabane have male unemployment rates reported to be in the region of 35 to 40 per cent. Over half of those unemployed have been so for over a year; this compares with roughly 40 per cent of the UK. Unemployment is also seen by many to be a sectarian issue. In 1991 Catholics are still at least twice as likely to be out of work as Protestants.

Agriculture and food is the largest industry in Northern Ireland. In terms of wealth creation, it is one of the best performing sectors, with an annual gross output of UK£1,300 million. Over 60 per cent of what is produced is exported and some 20 per cent of Northern Ireland's work-force is engaged directly or indirectly in agriculture. An increasing proportion of the rural labour force is not, however, engaged in full-time agricultural production. Farm-household incomes often depend on non-agricultural enterprises or employment. UK and EC agricultural policies are likely to accentuate these trends.

The impact of the changing rural economy is greatest on the Catholic community which, for historical reasons, generally owns poorer land. The plantations of the seventeenth century ensured that possession of the land would be a continuing sectarian issue. The divide is imperfectly reflected in the two largest agricultural organisations. The Ulster Farmers' Union, which represents larger farmers mostly in milk production, is disproportionately Protestant. On the other hand, the Northern Ireland Agricultural Producers' Association, which draws from smaller farmers more dependent on beef, especially in the western and border countries, is largely Catholic.

Because of its weak manufacturing base and high unemployment, the economy will continue to be dependent upon outside resources for some time to come: 'If forced to live within its means, Northern Ireland would experience a catastrophic fall in material living standards, which would fall to 60% of the present level or less.'[7]

The government of Northern Ireland

As a result of the Government of Ireland Act 1920, a wide range of responsibilities, including education, health, personal social services, law and order, housing, planning and economic development, amongst others, were devolved to the regional parliament and government at Stormont. Certain wider matters, such as foreign affairs, were not within the competence of the Northern Ireland parliament. A separate civil service – the Northern Ireland Civil Service (NICS) – was set up to help administer these functions. This structure survived until 1972, when the Northern Ireland parliament was prorogued and 'direct rule' was established. The NICS remained in place but its political direction comes from London-based ministers. The machinery of government and the delivery of public services are organised on a regional, sub-regional and local basis and direct rule did not alter this.

There are six statutory Northern Ireland government departments, the work of which includes co-ordinating the activities of sub-regional and local bodies. For example, housing policy, planning and other local services in general are the responsibility of the Department of Environment for Northern Ireland though the provision of public housing is not managed by it directly. Similarly, the Department of Education is responsible for oversight of the Education and Library Boards. Other parts of the Northern Ireland government include the Departments of Agriculture and of Economic Development (DED). The DED is responsible for the development of trade and industry, and for labour force matters such as industrial training and industrial relations. Other functions are also carried out by the DED in the areas of registration of companies, consumer protection and health and safety at work. The principal aims of the DED are to strengthen the Northern Ireland economy. The Department of Health and Social Services is very large and takes overall responsibility for all health and personal social services and social security matters. The central functions of the civil service are carried out by the Department of Finance and Personnel.

Table 7.1 *The Northern Ireland departments*

Department of Agriculture
Department of Economic Development
Department of Education
Department of Environment
Department of Finance and Personnel
Department of Health and Social Services

In addition to government departments there are a number of state bodies with specific tasks. For example, the Industrial Development Board (IDB), established in 1982, plays a leading role in the industrial development of Northern Ireland. The UK civil service also has local offices in Northern Ireland such as the Inland Revenue, Customs and Excise and the Stationery Office.

The Secretary of State for Northern Ireland, through the Northern Ireland Office, directs the work of Northern Ireland departments as well as dealing with matters reserved to the UK government such as law and order.

The politically sensitive provision of public housing is now controlled by the Northern Ireland Housing Executive. Health and personal social services are the responsibility of four sub-regional boards. Education is also administered on a sub-regional basis through five Education and Library Boards.

The Anglo-Irish Agreement established an Intergovernmental Conference through which the Irish government can put forward views on specified matters affecting Northern Ireland affairs and crossborder co-operation. The Conference, which has a secretariat in Belfast, meets regularly and is chaired jointly by the Secretary of State for Northern Ireland and the Minister for Foreign Affairs from Dublin. Among the Conference's concerns have been issues related to religious discrimination, extradition between the two jurisdictions, increasing the confidence of the Catholic community in the administration of justice and the promotion of equality in employment between Catholics and Protestants.

Local government

The Local Government (NI) Act 1972 provided for the creation of twenty-six local authorities with responsibilities for relatively few executive functions. These included:

(a) certain regulatory services, for example licensing of cinemas, dance-halls, building regulations and health inspection; and

(b) the provision of a limited range of services including street cleaning, refuse collection and disposal, burial grounds and crematoria, public baths, recreation facilities and tourist amenities.

Refuse collection and disposal and the provision of leisure and community services represent the major items of expenditure by local authorities in Northern Ireland. Local government expenditure overall is a relatively low proportion of public expenditure. In 1989–90 district council expenditure was under 3 per cent of total public expenditure in Northern Ireland, which amounted to over

UK£5 billion.

In addition to these executive responsibilities, local authorities have representative and consultative functions. Local authorities are entitled to representation on certain public agencies, advisory councils and the area boards. Local councils are also consulted about matters for which they have no executive responsibility such as proposed housing schemes, planning applications and road schemes within their area.

Elections to the local authorities are held every four years. After the May 1989 contest, eighteen of the twenty-six were controlled by parties favouring unionism, though various forms of 'power' or 'responsibility'-sharing are operated in these. A major feature of the 1989 elections were the impressive gains made by the SPLP, which increased by twenty its seats in councils. Sinn Féin's vote declined marginally but it lost sixteen seats. The presence on councils of open supporters of the IRA caused a great deal of resentment among Unionist councillors and much council business has been disrupted by protests at Sinn Féin's participation after the previous 1985 elections. Similarly, local councils have been the focus of Unionist protest at the signing of the Anglo-Irish Agreement. The 1989 election saw a movement away from the extremes both on the unionist and nationalist sides. Since the election, Unionists are increasingly returning to council business, and since 1989 all candidates have been required to renounce the use of violence for political ends. The local government system is the only one in Northern Ireland that permits locally-elected politicians a direct albeit limited policy-making role. It is likely, therefore, that despite a more constructive approach from many newly-elected councillors, it will continue to be in some degree of crisis until a wider political solution is available that commands sufficient consent in both communities.[8]

The effect of European Community membership

Attitudes to the European Community in Northern Ireland are ambivalent. Many Protestants are suspicious of what they perceive to be the Catholic ethos in Europe, the implicit dilution of UK

sovereignty and the opportunity it provides the Republic for
political advantage. On the other hand, the benefits of the
agricultural and regional policies are also acknowledged. The
European Community has been particularly active in promoting
development of the greater Belfast area. For nationalists, the
development of Europe, particularly the completion of the internal
market in 1992, will decrease the economic significance of the
border and make it harder for Unionists to deny the mutual
interests of the two parts of the island relative to Britain. The
European Regional Development Fund categorises both parts of
Ireland as areas in which government activity in economic development should be greatest.[9]

Towards a settlement

Direct rule from London is not seen by any of the main political
actors in Northern Ireland as a long-term solution to the conflict.
A variety of settlements has been suggested but none has com-
manded sufficient consent to succeed. In practice any proposed
internal Northern Ireland settlement can be vetoed if one community refuses to accept it.

For most people in Ireland the 'New Ireland Forum', which
met in Dublin in 1983, represented a major learning experience.
For many years, the underlying assumption of nationalists had
been that a united Ireland was the only solution. The Report of
the Forum, published in May 1984, set out the main options
which constitutional nationalists saw as open for discussion. The
Forum was made up of representatives of all those parties on the
island who opposed a violent solution, except the Unionist parties,
which refused to attend.

Sinn Féin, because it is regarded as a front for the IRA, was not
invited to participate. The options put forward in the Report
included the traditional unitary state, though few observers see
this as realistic. More interestingly, the Forum Report outlined
proposals for joint authority over Northern Ireland by Britain and
the Republic or some form of federal or confederate state. The
Forum Report's various options were dismissed rather pre-

emptorily by the UK government soon after their publication. Nevertheless they served as an opening agenda for serious discussion.

In November 1985 the British and Irish governments signed an agreement under which the Dublin authorities would be consulted on Northern affairs. The boost to the confidence of moderate Catholic opinion which the signing of the Anglo-Irish Agreement represented was considerable. After over sixty years of frustration and limited recognition of their tradition, the Unionist veto on progress had been removed. For Protestants the shock and dismay was profound. Their anger eventually led to street protests, strikes and civil disobedience. The two governments, however, remain committed to this internationally recognised treaty.

The Agreement allowed for an Intergovernmental Conference in which the Irish government would put forward views and proposals concerning stated aspects of Northern Ireland affairs and in which determined efforts would be made to resolve any differences between the two governments. The involvement of Dublin angered unionists but the Irish government's recognition of the status of Northern Ireland within the UK also upset die-hard nationalist opinion. The Agreement raised many expectations among Catholics that historic and recent grievances would be addressed. Progress towards the resolution of many problems has been slow, especially in the area of the administration of justice. Nevertheless, the Agreement has caused the Protestant community to search more earnestly for a compromise that would satisfy Catholics while defending their own interests. After much political manoeuvring, talks about the future government of Northern Ireland which were to involve the UK and Irish governments and those political parties in Northern Ireland who reject violent methods began in April 1991. Although a great many hopes for peace rested on the outcome the talks concluded in July without a settlement.

References

1 B. Purdie, 'Was the civil rights movement a Republican Communist conspiracy?', *Irish Political Studies*, 1988, Vol. 3, pp. 33–41.

2 Revd Ian Paisley, quoted in P. O'Malley, *The Uncivil War: Ireland Today*, Belfast: Blackstaff Press, 1983, p. 191.

3 Quoted in P. Buckland, *The Factory of Grievances. Devolved Government in Northern Ireland 1922-1939*, Dublin: Gill & Macmillan, 1979, p. 72.

4 D. Fell, 'Building a better economy', *TSB Economic and Business Review*, 1986, Vol. 1, No. 3, pp. 22–5.

5 Northern Ireland Economic Council, *Economic Assessment. Report 64*, 1987, p. 13.

6 B. Rowthorn, 'Northern Ireland: an economy in crisis', in P. Teague (ed.), *Beyond the Rhetoric, Politics, the Economy and Social Policy in Northern Ireland*, London: Lawrence & Wishart, 1987, p. 118.

7 Rowthorn, 'Northern Ireland: an economy in crisis'.

8 M. Connolly & C. Knox, 'Recent political difficulties of local government in N. Ireland', *Policy and Politics*, 1988, Vol. 16, No. 2, pp. 89-97.

9 J. Lodge (ed.), *Institutions of the European Community*, London: Croom Helm, 1987, p. 123.

Further reading

P. Arthur, *Government and Politics of Northern Ireland*, Harlow: Longman, 1987 (2nd edn).

P. Arthur & K. Jeffery, *Northern Ireland since 1968*, Oxford: Basil Blackwell, 1988.

M. Connolly, *Politics and Policy-making in Northern Ireland*, Hemel Hempstead: Philip Allen, 1990.

J. McGarry & B. O'Leary, *The Future of Northern Ireland*, Oxford: Clarendon Press, 1990.

J. Whyte, *Interpreting Northern Ireland*, Oxford: Oxford University Press, 1991.

8

EXTERNAL RELATIONS

Ireland's place in the world economic order, as discussed in Chapter 1, influences its relations with other countries to a very great degree. Countries with which Ireland has significant trading relations are obviously the object of much government and private attention. The recent rationalisation of Ireland's embassies, consulates and missions was guided in large part by the volume of trade currently conducted or likely to be carried out in the near future. Other factors are also important. These include the pattern of Irish migration in this and previous generations, the spread of Irish missionary efforts and the desire to forge a distinctive Irish foreign policy. In this chapter, the range of Ireland's relations with other countries is outlined, with special attention being paid to Britain, America, the EC, and the United Nations.

A feature of Irish foreign policy which marks it off either from Britain or America is its neutrality. Both Britain and America are parts of the North Atlantic Treaty Organisation (NATO), an alliance which was formed after the Second World War to resist any threat of Soviet expansion. Most of the members of NATO had been parties to the war, as were most of NATO's counterparts in the Warsaw Pact. Ireland had remained neutral following the outbreak of fighting in Europe in 1939 and this policy of neutrality was continued in the post-war years. Initially, the decision to remain neutral was in large part a by-product of Anglo-Irish relations. Though neutrality had been a recurring theme in nationalist thought for some time, in the late 1930s the Irish government saw the entering of an alliance involving the UK as incompatible with

Ireland's claim that Northern Ireland was part of the national territory. Although the original decision was in many ways a pragmatic one, the maintenance of the position of neutrality during and since the war has been seen by many people as an assertion and affirmation of the independence of the Irish state.

Relations with Britain

Ireland's relations with Britain are fashioned by a number of interrelated factors. The relationship between the neighbouring islands is complex, involved and multi-faceted. Many Irish people live in Britain, British companies have invested readily in Ireland and for many professional, cultural, sporting and other social organisations the two islands are treated jointly. The Republic is the only country with which the UK has a land border. When Ireland became a republic in 1948, it retained the most favoured nation-status usually accorded only to British Commonwealth nations and Irish citizens in Britain have never been treated as foreigners. Northern Ireland is an important issue in both countries and can always intrude into areas of policy, economic and social exchange which would otherwise develop more harmoniously.

The relations between Ireland and Britain are conditioned by a number of asymmetries of power. Britain is a large, highly economically developed state, which, while no longer the great power it was, participates much more centrally than Ireland in world affairs. The British political leadership sees its international role as a significant one in relation to world trade, nuclear disarmament and other military matters, scientific research and cultural endeavour. British diplomats, military personnel and business people are actively engaged in almost every major theatre of world affairs through treaty obligations, vestiges of colonial responsibilities and economic self-interest.

Many small countries with such powerful neighbours find it difficult to come to terms with their relatively minor place in the larger's world view. In Ireland's case, this difficulty is intensified by its former place in the British Empire. Ireland pursues an active foreign policy in areas of no immediate material advantage to it and often, though not necessarily deliberately, takes a contrary view on issues to the UK. Some observers feel that many aspects of Irish foreign policy arise from the need to assert the nation's status as an independent actor on the world stage. For Ireland, nationalism is the dominant ideology. It binds diverse individuals into 'a people', acts as a motive for economic, cultural and sporting achievement and provides a source of genuine pride and sympathy. The nation has become the highest affiliation and obligation of the individual and through it a significant part of personal identity is formed. For Irish people, however, much of the definition of that identity is found in relation to Britain. National achievement is frequently measured relative to Britain and to perform better than England in particular is sufficient to define success. This attitude is inevitably reflected in matters of public policy. Issues are defined in nationalist terms very readily and injustices, insults, ingratitude or ungraciousness to any one Irish person by Britain is seen as reflecting on all. British politicians and bureaucrats are often insensitive to Irish nationalism and, while they may well treat many other groups equally badly, in Ireland such actions tend to be seen as reflecting national antagonism, disrespect or disinterest.

Relations between Britain and Ireland are complicated by the asymmetry of attention each pays to the other. In Britain, domestic Irish politics not relating directly to Northern Ireland get similar coverage in the media to that given to France or Germany, perhaps less. By contrast, not only does the Irish media devote considerable space to British affairs but British television and newspapers are freely and widely available. The reverse is not true. The Irish public is more attentive to, and informed about, events in Britain than any other country with which Ireland has direct dealings. This high level of British media penetration is reinforced by the ready movement of Irish people to Britain for business and other reasons. The easy communications between Ireland and Britain help solidify the generally favourable image of British people in Ireland. These attitudes do not extend, however, to the British government and 'Establishment'. Images of British institutions as opposed to individuals are mediated by the predominant nationalistic historical interpretation of the British role in denying Ireland's independence. As a result, Irish public policy to Britain is officially cautious, occasionally suspicious and always watchful. At the same time, senior politicians and public officials enjoy useful, regular and friendly relations with their British counterparts. British ideas, laws, enquiries and reports are certainly the most pervasive and persuasive outside influences on Irish politics today.

Relations with the USA

Irish political relations with America have much to do with Anglo-Irish relations. The USA, with its substantial ethnic Irish community, has often been viewed as a potentially powerful ally in arguments with Britain on aspects of administration in Northern Ireland. Such an outlook is ironic in that British politicians have since 1945 laid great stress on their 'special relationship' with America. The attitudes of Irish Americans, particularly those who identify emotionally with Ireland, are heavily tutored by their forefathers' experience of rural Ireland under British political and landlord rule and of America as poor emigrants. For Irish Americans who have not prospered, Britain remains a *bête noire*. Even among those who have enjoyed social and economic success in America, old images remain important. Many Irish Americans do not have sustained, personal and direct experience of Ireland. As a result Irish-American sentiment, money and influence have often been used in ways which Irish governments find unhelpful. Much of Ireland's considerable diplomatic effort in America has been directed to 're-educating' American opinion. That opinion is often much more intensely anti-British than domestic opinion. Irish Americans may be persuaded more easily that the IRA is a liberating force standing between the nationalist community in Northern Ireland and British repression than voters in the Republic.

Official Irish relations with the USA have been markedly aided in recent years by the active involvement of 'The Friends of Ireland', a group of Democratic and Republican congressmen and senators. The Friends have worked closely with Irish diplomats to

assist the Irish government's case for peaceful reform in Northern
Ireland and an end to private American financial support for the
IRA. Other Irish-American groups, notably Noraid, the Irish
National Caucus and the *ad hoc* Congressional committee, seek to
advance more radical and republican interpretations of events in
Northern Ireland. These elements have had a number of successes
in persuading American politicians, especially in state legislatures,
to adopt measures on extradition and conditions for American
investment in Northern Ireland which British governments oppose. The impact on American investment of such action is
minimal. Occasionally, the Irish-American lobby works in close
harmony, as during the debate on ratifying the US–UK extradition treaty which came into force in December 1986 after an
embarrassingly long legislative delay.

Irish political influence on American policy is greatest in the
legislature rather than the executive. While it is no longer
important which party has the presidency, there are barriers to
Irish influence. Britain's sway in the State Department (the
American department of foreign affairs) and the Department of
Defence has always been sufficient to counter any unwelcome
Irish manoeuvre. Although Irish neutrality during the Second
World War has faded as a contentious issue, Britain's centrality to
American intelligence-gathering and other military involvements
continues to be crucial. Further, the extensive economic and
financial links between the USA and Britain are a significant
factor in ensuring that the two countries' relations remain har-
monious in political terms.

Irish interests clash occasionally with those of ethnic American
groups, particularly in recent years, on the issue of the reform of
US immigration laws. The Irish lobby in Washington has had to
work very hard to convince the US legislature to support measures in this area which would give Irish applicants for US visas a
more reasonable chance of success. Other ethnic interests are keen
to ensure that any concession to Ireland would not be at their
expense. On the whole however, Irish-American relations are very
close, usually becoming contentious only when British interests
are at issue. They are likely to improve further if Ireland continues

to be an attractive location for American investment. Ireland retains important resources of goodwill, emotion and mutual economic self-interest in the USA.

Relations within the European Community

Ireland's entry to the European Community in 1973 was heralded by many as a chance to lessen decisively the influence of Britain on Irish life. It has indeed had a major impact and Irish enthusiasm for Europe remains high. For a small state with a relatively open economy, participation in the Community has meant great economic opportunities and unusual political influence. When Ireland holds the presidency of Europe, Irish ministers play a more significant role on the world stage. At the same time Irish businessmen and public servants have seen the European Community as an opportunity to develop their talents in a wider setting than before. There has been some resistance to the EC from groups who fear a loss of Irish sovereignty but overall Ireland has seen itself as being an enthusiastic, co-operative and active Community member.

Since accession to the EC, Ireland has received considerable financial transfers from Community funds. In fact approximately 8 per cent of the government's current budget comes from Brussels. Irish officials have been vigorous and assiduous in gaining funds. To an extent, public policy in Ireland is EC-led, in that some programmes and projects are given particular priority because funding is available for them. Ireland's interests in Brussels are, like all member states, looked after by the country's Permanent Representation, a body akin to an embassy, which services important committees, particularly one known by its French language initials as COREPER. In addition, Irish ministers and officials attend numerous EC meetings ranging from the weekly management meeting to regulate certain farm commodities to those of the European Council itself. As was seen in Chapter 2, Community legislation, known as directives and regulations, has a considerable impact on domestic policies, often in areas where Irish policy was previously under-developed.

The progress of European integration has until recently been intergovernmental rather than supra-national. Thus, Irish governments have been able to participate in Community policy-making on a relatively advantageous footing, given the size of Ireland's population. Certainly, Irish ministers see their position as one among twelve as an advantage not enjoyed by Ireland's Members of the European Parliament, where the whole island has only eighteen seats among 518. Conversely, in the system of qualified majority voting used for most issues in the European Council, Ireland cast only three of the seventy-six votes, with fifty-four needed for a decision. In the European Parliament, members from the Republic are found in seven of the ten political groups and can, therefore, call on considerable support on issues of importance to Ireland.

The development of the European Community following the Single European Act and in the preparations for the completion of the internal market in 1992 is problematic for Ireland. Many more decisions can now be made on a Community level despite national reservations. The pace of change is, therefore, set to increase. Further, the European Commission is now intent in some policy areas on building up relations with public authorities at sub-national level rather than through central government. For Ireland, where regional and even local institutions are weak, such a development represents a major challenge to established political and administrative practice. To gain maximum benefits, however, from the EC as it prepares for 1992, more radical decentralisation of power than that outlined in Chapter 6 may be necessary.

At the meeting of the European Council in Dublin in June 1990, agreement was reached to convene twin intergovernmental conferences to examine the issue of economic and monetary, and political union, with the aim of ratification of the results by member states by the end of 1992. Potentially the most important change for Ireland consequent on the further integration of the European Community are moves to develop a European defence and/or foreign policy. Although Irish governments have sought to avoid the two issues becoming interconnected, European political co-ordination as it may evolve and Irish neutrality in its present form may be incompatible. Already politicians in the major parties have taken sharply opposing stances on neutrality. The Single European Act contains no obligation to military co-operation but it does formalise a long-standing arrangement known as European Political Co-operation (EPC). Already the EC foreign ministers try to co-ordinate foreign policy positions. This has involved common declarations on South Africa, Central America and the Middle East. Irish ministers have from time to time had to remind EPC meetings of the convention that political and economic but not military security questions can be raised.

Both proponents and opponents of Irish neutrality see this distinction as likely to be put under considerable pressure as the EC develops common economic, trade and related social policies. Opponents of neutrality say that Ireland should not attempt to hold back the development of a common EC defence policy. Defence of Europe is a moral obligation for countries seeking its benefits and, in any case, the other member states will grow impatient with Ireland's singular stance. Those who favour neutrality point to the benefits to Europe and even to the rest of the world of at least one member of the Community being neutral. Further, any move into closer defence arrangements with other member states would draw Ireland closer to the NATO defence pact which involves wider and even less attractive obligations. The debate on neutrality has not fully developed to date but it is likely to become more intense as Ireland's relations with the EC become even closer.

Relations with the United Nations

Despite the attempts of EPC to reach a common position on various issues, Ireland's neutrality frequently puts it in a minority position within the twelve-member EC block in the United Nations (UN). All EC member-states vote more often with the US than Ireland, except for Greece. In recent years Ireland was in a minority in relation to the EC block on disarmament issues and apartheid. Nevertheless, the EPC has reduced the scope of Ireland's UN role which, prior to accession to the EC, was less constrained by material European interests.

Ireland's activist and enthusiastic stance in relation to international organisations such as the UN began in the 1920s and 1930s. The Free State's membership of the League of Nations was an important assertion of nationhood. De Valera, in particular, ensured that Ireland's voice was heard in the 1930s when Italy's and Germany's military policies were disturbing the world order. Ireland was excluded from the United Nations until 1955 because of a Soviet veto. Again de Valera's government, returned in 1957, signalled an activist stance on issues such as China's representation at the UN, arms control and disarmament. In the League and the UN, Ireland has been a strong advocate of giving maximum authority to the world body in settling disputes. Despite the opposition of groups apprehensive about the maintenance of neutrality, Ireland allowed US planes bound for the 1990 war with Iraq to refuel at Shannon airport because the American action had UN authority. Ireland is also strongly committed to UN peace-keeping and has sent troops to the Congo, Cyprus, Lebanon, Sinai and recently, the Iran/Iraq border. Irish people in general have taken pride in the military role afforded by the UN.

Interested pressure groups, such as those concerned with development aid, have looked to the UN delegation to speak out on Third World issues. Ireland's contribution to the debate in the UN on international issues is seldom of broad domestic interest except on occasions, such as the various meetings during the Falkland/Malvinas crisis, when Irish 'independence' caused offence to Britain. Critics of Irish foreign policy view the assertion of national independence through clashes with Britain as short-sighted and unwise. Such commentators acknowledge that Ireland's reputation in the Third World and elsewhere may be enhanced, but point to the more immediate benefits of EC solidarity and good relations with a powerful neighbour.

Other external commitments

As was seen in Chapter 2, Ireland has another important European commitment outside the EC. The European Convention for the

Protection of Human Rights and Fundamental Freedoms (1950) is one of the most important of a large number of international declarations of rights made since 1945. In contrast with the United Nations' Universal Declaration of Human Rights (1947), and the subsequent UN charters of rights, the European Convention has an important element of collective enforcement.

Ireland adopted the Convention in November 1950 and it came into force in September 1953. Along with most other European countries, Ireland accepted an optional clause of the Convention which permits citizens to petition directly to the European Commission on Human Rights, which can take cases to the Committee of Ministers of the Council of Europe and then (given a two-thirds majority on the Council) to the European Court of Human Rights. This is a course of action which has been used successfully in a number of cases involving Ireland. All the protocols of the Convention have been signed except that covering the death penalty for certain offences about which Ireland, Germany, Belgium and several other countries have particular reservations. Other parts of the Convention were signed but only ratified in 1989.

Since the late 1950s, Ireland has been a member of many major international organisations such as the International Monetary Fund, the International Bank for Reconstruction and Development, the International Finance Corporation and the International Development Association. Ireland is a founder member of the Organisation for Economic Co-operation and Development (OECD) The OECD and its affiliated organisations assist the twenty-four member countries' governments with the formulation of economic and social policy. Its reports are often the focus of debate in Ireland because of their wide comparative analysis and authoritative style.

In common with other countries Ireland uses its assistance to developing countries as part of its foreign policy. Ireland spends in the region of IR£40 million per year on development assistance to Third World countries. Approximately 40 per cent of this total is spent on bilateral assistance (direct Irish aid to developing countries) and the rest is given to international organisations to support their development activities. Over 60 per cent of bilateral aid is spent in projects in Ireland's four priority countries, Lesotho, Tanzania, Zambia and the Sudan, the largest sectors of expenditure being agricultural and rural development, education and training.

Conclusions

As is the case in many other countries, external relations are often discussed in Ireland in terms of sovereignty. The idea that a nation–state should have power and control over its own future is very strongly held. In reality, Ireland is as constrained in foreign affairs as it is in other areas of policy by its position in the world economy and by the tight network of international obligations, organisations and agreements in which all modern countries operate. Indeed, while the Republic of Ireland now has all the symbols of independence, the level of its interdependence with the rest of the world has never been greater. Nation-states no longer have complete and actual control over the direction of policy in their own territory even if they do so formally. There are clearly difficulties, therefore, in analysing external relations in terms of purely formal sovereignty.

The world economic system serves to limit the autonomy of national governments. In Chapter 1, we examined Ireland's place in the international division of labour and saw that it competed with other semi-peripheral countries for international investment. A key role in this global system is played by multinational companies for which national boundaries are less important than comparative costs and opportunities. For such companies, technological advances in communications and transportation have eroded the relevance of independent national economic policies. Ireland's foreign policy is aimed in part to protect the Irish economy from the vagaries of the world economic order by co-operating with other countries for the co-ordination of policy. To an extent, therefore, the notion of sovereignty can only really be understood in terms of foreign policies aimed at collective action by states rather than internal national control. The year 1992 – the date set for removal of all trade barriers in the EC – will make a further diminution of sovereignty as it has been popularly understood.

Irish foreign policy may have to come to terms with greater European co-operation on defence with the obvious difficulties for the policy of neutrality. The pressure for a European defence is itself a product of the changes within the hegemonic power blocs which dominate world politics. All of Ireland's EC partners are part of alliance which limits them as autonomous military actors. NATO nations do retain the capacity for independent military action but they also recognise the reality of collective security. Although not all NATO countries participate fully, the existence of an integrated supranational command structure ensures that in certain military crises 'national armies' would operate within the framework of the supreme allied command. Given that its partners have qualified their national sovereignty in the name of collective defence, it is likely that this is the model which would be used to shape any specifically EC security arrangements. More importantly, however, the doubts about American commitment, the East—West negotiations on conventional forces in Europe and political ferment in Eastern Europe will present the countries of Western Europe with new political and military choices for which Ireland may have to assume some responsibility.

The rapidly changing context in which Ireland arranges its external relations involves the world economic order, international treaties, other countries' arrangements for collective defence, international law and the EC. All of these may appear to erode Ireland's independence of action or sovereignty. In fact, however, many of the obligations and constraints represent an enhancement of Ireland's potential as an economic and political actor. The EC, in particular, protects the national economy, environment and human potential. It allows Ireland to make a more significant impact on world developments than it otherwise could.

Further reading

P. Arthur, *Aspirations and Assertions: Britain, Ireland and the Northern Ireland Problem*, London: Routledge, 1991.

P. Keatinge, *A Singular Stance: Irish Neutrality in the 1980s*, Dublin: Institute of Public Administration, 1984.

P. Keatinge (ed.), *Ireland and EC Membership Evaluated*, London: Frances Pinter, 1991.

KEY FACTS

Party leaders, 1922-91

Fianna Fáil

Eamon de Valera	1926–59
Seán Lemass	1959–66
Jack Lynch	1966–79
Charles Haughey	1979– .

Cumann na nGaedheal

William T. Cosgrave	1923–33

Fine Gael

Eoin O'Duffy	1933–34
William T. Cosgrave	1935–44
Richard Mulcahy	1944–59
James Dillon	1959–65
Liam Cosgrave	1965–77
Garret FitzGerald	1977–87
Alan Dukes	1987–90
John Bruton	1990–

Labour Party

Thomas Johnson	1918–27
T. J. O'Connell	1927–32
William Norton	1932–61
Brendan Corish	1961–77
Frank Cluskey	1977–81
Michael O'Leary	1981–82
Dick Spring	1982–

Heads of state and of govermnents, 1922-91

Heads of state	*Heads of government*
Irish Free State:	Irish Free State:
King (through Governor-General)	President of the Executive Council
T. Healy (1922-28)	W.T. Cosgrave (1922-32)
J. MacNeill (1928-32)	
D. O'Buachalla (1932-36)	E. de Valera (1932-37)
Ireland:	Ireland:
President	Taoiseach
D. Hyde (1938-45)	E. de Valera (1937-48)
	J. Costello (1948-51)
S. T. O'Ceallaigh (1945-59)	E. de Valera (1951-54)
	J. Costello (1954-57)
	E. de Valera (1957-59)
E. de Valera (1959-73)	S. Lemass (1959-66)
	J. Lynch (1966-73)
E. Childers (1973-74)	L. Cosgrave (1973-77)
C. O Dalaigh (1974-76)	J. Lynch (1977-79)
P. Hillery (1976-90)	C. Haughey (1979-81)
M. Robinson (1990-)	G. FitzGerald (1981-82)
	C. Haughey (1982-82)
	G. FitzGerald (1982-87)
	C. Haughey (1987-)

State of the parties in parliament

Daíl Eireann (1.1.89)		Westminster (1.1.89)	
Fianna Fáil	81	Official Unionists	9
Fine Gael	51	Democratic Unionists	3
Progressive Democrats	14	Popular Unionists	1
Labour	12	SDLP	3
Workers' Party	4	Sinn Féin	1
Others	4		
Vacant	0		

Electoral system

Elections in the Republic and Northern Ireland (except those in the UK parliament at Westminster) are conducted under a system of proportional representation (PR). The PR systems are used in many countries but the version established in Ireland is called the Single Transferable Vote (STV) in multi-member constituencies. Here is an example of an STV contest:

The election to the European Parliament in Northern Ireland in 1984

Electorate 1,065,353; valid vote 685,317; spoiled votes 11,654; percentage poll 65.42%; quota 171,330.

First count

I. Paisley (DUP)	230,251
J. Hume (SDLP)	151,399
J.Taylor(Off.Un)	147,169
D. Morrison (SF)	91,476
D. Cook (All)	34,046
J. Kilfedder (Ass. Speaker)	20,092
S. Lynch (WP)	8,712
C. McGuigan (Ecology)	2,172

Elected: Ian Paisley

Second count
Distribution of Paisley's surplus
and Kilfedder's votes

Hume	(+265)	151,665
Taylor	(+38,545)	185,714
Morrison	(+49)	91,525
Cook	(+846)	34,892
Kilfedder	(+18,201)	38,293
Lynch	(+101)	8,813
McGuigan	(+64)	2,236

Elected: John Taylor
Eliminated McGuigan and Lynch

Third count
Distribution of Lynch's
and McGuigan's votes

Hume	(+4,646)	156,310
Morrison	(+1,119)	92,644
Cook	(+2,509)	37,401
Kilfedder	(+560)	38,854

No candidate reached quota
Eliminated: Kilfedder and Cook

Fourth count
Distribution of Cook's

Hume (+26,946)	183,256
Morrison (+435)	93,080

Elected: John Hume

Method of voting

Each voter is given a ballot paper with a list of the names of the individual candidates in alphabetical order. The candidate's party affiliation, if any, is also on the ballot paper. The voter then ranks the candidates on a 1,2,3, etc., basis in order of preference. There is no obligation to express more than a first preference. On the other hand, the voter is free to give a vote to as many candidates as he/she chooses provided that he/she does so in an unbroken sequence of preferences. The outcome of an STV election depends on a process of counting preferences and transferring votes. Successful candidates are those who reach the 'quota'. This is calculated by dividing the valid votes by one more than the number of seats to be filled, and to the result of that division adding 1. In our example, 685,317 votes were divided by 4 (ie. 3 for the seats available plus 1) to give 171,329, then 1 was added to establish the quota.

Once a candidate has reached the quota, as Ian Paisley did at the first count, his extra votes are shared out among the other candidates according to the voters' preference. Then the process is repeated, with some candidates being eliminated as 'no-hopers', until all the seats are filled. The process often appears complicated to an outside observer. From the voters' point of view, however, the system is simple. It allows individual electors to vote exclusively for one party or for several parties. If the parties put up a variety of candidates in terms of age, sex, occupation or other characteristics they may think important, a voter may seek to influence the outcome by distributing preferences according to those aspects considered most important. Many Irish voters favour candidates who live in their immediate area or with whose families they have some connections (see Chapter 2).

Glossary

Some Irish terms are used in everyday speech in Ireland. Below are the rough translations of some of the most common.

Ard-Fheis The annual conference of a political party.

Bunreacht na hEireann The Constitution of Ireland. This term is usually applied only to the Constitution enacted in 1937 and still in
force.

Ceann Comhairle Speaker of the Dáil.

Dáil (full title, *Dáil Eireann)* Chamber of Deputies. The popularly
elected legislative assembly. Lower house of the Irish
Parliament, the *Oireachtas.*

Eire Ireland. Often used inaccurately outside Ireland as the name
of the twenty-six-county state.

Fianna Fáil The largest party in Ireland, founded by Eamon de
Valera in 1926, currently led by Charles Haughey.

Fine Gael The successor of Cumann na nGaedheal (literally
League of Gaels), the pro-Treaty party. The second largest
party in Ireland, currently led by John Bruton.

Garda Síochána The Guards or Police.

Oireachtas The whole parliament – President, Dáil and Seanad.

Seanad or *Seanad Eireann* The Senate.

Sinn Féin Originally a nationalist political movement founded by
Arthur Griffith in 1905. The movement split over the terms of
the Treaty with the UK (December 1921). Organisations
calling themselves Sinn Féin have existed ever since but enjoy
little electoral support outside Northern Ireland.

Tanaiste Deputy Prime Minister.

Taoiseach Prime Minister.

Teachta Dála Deputy or member of parliament, usually
abbreviated to TD.

Demanded by Northern Ireland Civil Right Association, 1968

1 One person, one vote in local council elections.
2 An end to 'gerrymandered' electoral boundaries.
3 An end to discrimination by local government.
4 A points system for housing allocation.
5 Repeal of the Special Powers Act which allowed the police
   to detain without trial.
6 The disbanding of the B-Specials, a Protestant part-time
   force of armed police auxiliaries.

Stormont Prime Ministers, 1921-72

1921-41	James Craig	(Unionist)
1941-43	John Andrews	(Unionist)
1943-63	Basil Brooke	(Unionist)
1963-69	Terence O'Neill	(Unionist)
1969-71	James Chichester-Clark	(Unionist)
1971-72	Brian Faulkner	(Unionist)

British Secretaries of State for Northern Ireland

1972-73	William Whitelaw	(Conservative)
1973-74	Francis Pym	(Conservative)
1974-76	Merlyn Rees	(Labour)
1976-79	Roy Mason	(Labour)
1979-81	Humphrey Atkins	(Conservative)
1981-84	James Prior	(Conservative)
1984-85	Douglas Hurd	(Conservative)
1985-89	Tom King	(Conservative)
1989-	Peter Brooke	(Conservative)

Republic of Ireland

Population	3,503m (1990 est.)
Area	70,000 sq. km.
Density	51 per sq. km.
Gross National Product	IR£20,879bn (1989)*
Gross Domestic Product	IR£23,919bn (1989)*
	(67% of EC average)
Total labour force	1.12m (incl. unemployed; excl. first job-seekers) (1989)
Total at work	0.96m. (1989)

IR£ = UK£0.90 (at 4 April 1991)
IR£ = US$1-60
* at current market prices

Dates and events

432	St Patrick arrives to convert the pagan Irish kings.
1170	Norman/English conquest begins.
1558	Accession of Elizabeth I marks permanent identification of ruling English with Reformation.
1603	English law enforced throughout Ireland.
1606	Plantation of Ulster.
1690	Battle of Boyne marks defeat of Catholic counter-coup.
1695	First penal laws against Catholics enacted.
1796	French aid fails to help Irish rebels.
1798	Wolfe Tone attempts to overthrow British rule.
1800	Ireland governed through Irish Chief Secretary. Act of Union.
1803	Further rising fails.
1828	Election of Daniel O'Connell for County Clare forces consideration of granting Catholics right to sit in Westminster Parliament.
1829	Catholic Emancipation Act passed under pressure of mounting civil unrest.
1845	Famine begins.
1867	Further rising fails.
1879	Heightened rural agitation (Land War).
1886	First Home Rule Bill defeated in UK parliament.
1893	Second Home Rule Bill defeated.
1911	Carson unites Ulster resistance to Home Rule.
1912	Third Home Rule Bill passed.
1913	Ulster Protestant civil and armed resistance beings. Ulster Covenant signed by 250,000 people.
1914	Outbreak of First World War.
1916	Easter Rising
1918	Nationalists (Sinn Féin) gain major electoral victory.
1919	Alternative parliament (Dáil Eireann) set up in Dublin in midst of the War of Independence.
1921	Anglo-Irish Treaty, Ireland partitioned. Northern Ireland Parliament opened with large Unionist majority.

1922   Irish Free State formed. Civil War starts.

1923   Civil War ends.

1927   Defeated side in Civil War enter Dáil Eireann.

1937   New Irish constitution adopted.

1939   UK declares war on Germany.
        Ireland remains neutral.

1948   Republic of Ireland declared.

1956   IRA campaign renewed in Northern Ireland.

1962   IRA campaign called off.

1965   Exchange of visits by Taoiseach and Northern Irish
        prime minister.

1967   Civil Rights Association founded in Northern Ireland.

1969   British troops arrive to quell increasing unrest in
        Northern Ireland.

1972   Ireland joins the European Community.
        Direct rule from London introduced to Northern
        Ireland.
        Troops kill 13 protest marchers in Derry.

1973   Sunningdale agreement leads to power-sharing
        executive.

1974   Ulster Workers' Strike forces collapse of power-sharing
        executive.

1981   Hunger strike by Republican prisoners: 10 die.

1985   Anglo-Irish Agreement: consultative role for Dublin in
        Northern Ireland.

1987   Single European Act extends and modified impact of
        EC membership.

1990   Mary Robinson, first woman elected as President of
        Ireland.

1991   Inter-party talks in Northern Ireland under Secretary of
        State's initiative.
        Terrorist-related deaths in Northern Ireland since 1970
        reach 1,974 civilians (including terrorists), 907 security
        force members (June).

Percentage of First Preference votes (and seats in) in the Republic of Ireland General Elections of 1992 and 1989

Fianna Fail	39.1	(68)	44.1	(77)
Fine Gael	24.5	(45)	29.3	(55)
Labour	19.3	(33)	9.5	(15)
Progressive Democrats	4.7	(10)	5.0	(6)
Democratic Left	2.8	(4)	N/A	(N/A)
Workers Party	0.7	(–)	5.5	(7)
Independent & Others	8.9	(6)	6.6	(6)

Summary of the Fianna Fail/Labour 'Agreed Programme' for Government, 1993

* Creation of 30,000 new jobs a year
* Improved tax relief for mortgage holders
* Reduced hospital waiting lists
* New local authority housing starts
* Reduce pupil/teacher ratio
* Radical measures to fight crime
* A light rail system for Dublin
* Creation of a state bank
* Establish Department of Enterprise and Employment
* Establish Department of Tourism and Foreign Trade
* May day as public holiday
* Family law reform

Major Cabinet Posts in Fianna Fail/Labour Governemt, 1993

Taoiseach	Albert Reynolds (FF)
Tanaiste and Minister for Foreign Affairs	Dick Spring (Lab)
Minister for Finance	Bertie Ahern (FF)
Minister for Education	Niamh Bhreathnach (Lab)

There are 9 Fianna Fail and 6 Labour cabinet members

The result of the 1992 General Election of Northern Ireland

Party	Share of the vote (%)	Change from 1987 (%)	MPs elected	Change from 1987
United Ulster Unionist	34.8	–3.0	9	0
Democratic Unionist	13.1	+1.4	3	0
Ulster Popular Unionist	2.6	0.0	1	0
Alliance	8.7	–1.3	0	0
Social and Democratic Labour	23.5	+2.4	4	+1
Sin Fein	10.0	–1.4	0	–1
Others*	7.4	+2.0	0	0

*Includes Conservative Party of Northern Ireland, which obtained 6.7% of the total vote, Workers (0.6%), Natural Law (0.3%) and 'Others' (1.2%)

INDEX